Florida Legal Research

Carolina Academic Press
Legal Research Series

Suzanne E. Rowe, Series Editor
ta.

Arizona, Second Edition—Tamara S. Herrera

Arkansas—Coleen M. Barger

California, Second Edition—Hether C. Macfarlane, Aimee Dudovitz
& Suzanne E. Rowe

Colorado—Robert Michael Linz

Connecticut—Jessica G. Hynes

Federal—Mary Garvey Algero, Spencer L. Simons, Suzanne E. Rowe,
Scott Childs & Sarah E. Ricks

Florida, Fourth Edition—Barbara J. Busharis, Jennifer LaVia
& Suzanne E. Rowe

Georgia—Nancy P. Johnson, Elizabeth G. Adelman & Nancy J. Adams

Idaho—Tenielle Fordyce-Ruff & Suzanne E. Rowe

Illinois, Second Edition—Mark E. Wojcik

Iowa—John D. Edwards, M. Sara Lowe, Karen L. Wallace
& Melissa H. Weresh

Kansas—Joseph A. Custer & Christopher L. Steadham

Kentucky—William A. Hilyerd, Kurt X. Metzmeier & David J. Ensign

Louisiana, Second Edition—Mary Garvey Algero

Massachusetts—E. Joan Blum

Michigan, Second Edition—Pamela Lysaght & Cristina D. Lockwood

Minnesota—Suzanne Thorpe

Mississippi—Kristy L. Gilliland

Missouri, Second Edition—Wanda M. Temm & Julie M. Cheslik

New York, Second Edition—Elizabeth G. Adelman, Theodora Belniak
& Suzanne E. Rowe

North Carolina, Second Edition—Scott Childs & Sara Sampson

Ohio—Katherine L. Hall & Sara Sampson

Oklahoma—Darin K. Fox, Darla W. Jackson & Courtney L. Selby

Oregon, Third Edition—Suzanne E. Rowe

Pennsylvania—Barbara J. Busharis & Bonny L. Tavares

Tennessee—Sibyl Marshall & Carol McCrehan Parker

Texas, Revised Printing—Spencer L. Simons

Washington, Second Edition—Julie Heintz-Cho, Tom Cobb
& Mary A. Hotchkiss

West Virginia—Hollee Schwartz Temple

Wisconsin—Patricia Cervenka & Leslie Behroozi

Wyoming—Debora A. Person & Tawnya K. Plumb
ta.

Florida Legal Research

Fourth Edition

Barbara J. Busharis
Jennifer LaVia
Suzanne E. Rowe

Suzanne E. Rowe, Series Editor

CAROLINA ACADEMIC PRESS

Durham, North Carolina

Library of Congress Cataloging-in-Publication Data

Busharis, Barbara J., 1962- author.
 Florida legal research / Barbara J. Busharis, Jennifer LaVia, and Suzanne E.
Rowe. -- Fourth Edition.
     pages cm. -- (Legal research series)
 Includes bibliographical references and index.
 ISBN 978-1-61163-157-9 (alk. paper)
 1. Legal research--Florida. I. Lavia, Jennifer, author. II. Rowe, Suzanne E.,
1961- author. III. Title.

 KFF75.R69 2014
 340.072'0759--dc23

                        2014019461

CAROLINA ACADEMIC PRESS
700 Kent Street
Durham, North Carolina 27701
Telephone (919) 489-7486
Fax (919) 493-5668
www.cap-press.com

Printed in the United States of America
2018 Printing

Summary of Contents

Contents

List of Tables and Figures

Tables

Figures

Series Note

The Legal Research Series published by Carolina Academic Press includes titles from states around the country as well as a separate text on federal legal research. The goal of each book is to provide law students, practitioners, paralegals, college students, laypeople, and librarians with the essential elements of legal research in each jurisdiction. Unlike more bibliographic texts, the Legal Research Series books seek to explain concisely both the sources of legal research and the process for conducting legal research effectively.

Preface and Acknowledgments

The fourth edition of *Florida Legal Research* continues to fill a niche between general legal research textbooks and bibliographies specific to Florida. Reflecting the many changes in legal research since the third edition was published in 2007, this new edition has been extensively revised. We expanded treatment of online research using Lexis Advance, WestlawNext, free or low-cost providers, and governmental websites. We reorganized the chapters to cover the process of legal research and methods for organizing research at the beginning of the book. And we replaced a chapter on looseleaf services (now called "practice area services") with a new chapter including a variety of practice tools, including blogs. The last chapter provides an overview of current citation rules for Florida sources, reflecting recent changes in *The Bluebook: A Uniform System of Citation* and the *ALWD Citation Guide*.

As with prior editions, work on each chapter was collaborative, but we specifically recognize the contributions of our new co-author, Jennifer LaVia, in updating and modifying the current chapters on administrative law, secondary sources, practice aids, and court rules. We also acknowledge that portions of this book have appeared in prior editions (e.g., the research notebook explanation in Chapter 1 is drawn from Lisa Kuhlman Tietig's explanation in the first edition) and in other books in the Legal Research Series (e.g., the discussion of citators in Chapter 9 mirrors the treatment of citators in *Oregon Legal Research*).

We gratefully acknowledge the assistance and online materials provided by the Florida State University College of Law Research Center, especially the help of Margaret Clark, Katie Crandall, Katie Miller, and Stephanie Hayes. In Oregon, we were fortunate to have research, editorial, and administrative assistance from Kyung Duk Ko and Nicole Mortemore. We received quick and helpful responses to many queries about Lexis Advance from Megan McCombs Hays and about WestlawNext from Jessica Greathouse. Jay LaVia reviewed the chapter on administrative law materials with a practitioner's eye and made numerous helpful suggestions. We continue to be grateful for the feedback we receive from colleagues at various Florida law schools.

Finally, for their love (always) and understanding (mostly) when publishing deadlines took priority over family time, we thank Stan, Aidan, and Ethan Tozer; Jay, Hanna, and J.T. LaVia; and Mark Corley.

Barbara J. Busharis
Jennifer LaVia
Suzanne E. Rowe

Florida Legal Research

Introduction

The Legal Research Process

Legal research is a process. It has a logical sequence of steps with definite goals. The sequence of steps is not exactly the same for each research project, but the goals are the same. Viewing research as a process develops the critical skills needed to conduct thorough legal research, which will give you confidence in your ability to resolve legal issues.

The ultimate goal of legal research is to find primary authority that applies to the issue you have been asked to address. *Primary authority* is the law that controls the case. The three types of primary authority are judicial opinions, statutes and constitutions, and administrative regulations. Primary authority is the product of the three branches of government. Judicial opinions, or cases, are written decisions of courts determining the outcome of litigation. Statutes and constitutions are sometimes referred to as enacted law because they result from actions of legislatures. Administrative regulations are promulgated by agencies in the executive branch of government, such as the Florida Department of Environmental Protection. Administrative law includes the decisions of agencies that interpret regulations and apply them in contested situations; these decisions are similar to judicial opinions.

One step in every research process is determining which type or types of primary authority control the issue — cases, statutes and constitutions, or administrative regulations. Often, two or more of these types of primary authority work together to control an issue of law. Furthermore, you must determine whether federal law, state law, or both control the issue. Unless you are already very familiar with an area of law, answering these questions usually requires background research.

Secondary authority is a source that explains or interprets primary authority, but is not binding law. For example, a treatise may give a thorough summary of an area of law, but the treatise is only secondary authority, not binding law. Similarly, a law review article about a specific case may provide an ex-

3

cellent interpretation of the case, but only the case itself is binding law. Another example of a secondary source is a legal encyclopedia. Secondary sources are especially helpful to novice researchers because they can provide a broad overview of an unfamiliar area of law. This context often speeds research in primary authority.

This Introduction provides a very general overview of the research process that will be developed in the remainder of this book. There are four major steps in researching a legal issue: A) identifying the legal terms that will allow you to research the issue; B) using secondary sources to better understand the context of the issue; C) finding primary authority; and D) updating your research. The steps are not linear, and the order in which you take them will vary from one research project to another. Comprehensive research, however, requires attention to all four of these steps.

I. Overview of the Research Process

A. Identify the Issue and Related Research Terms

Sometimes you will research an issue that has already been defined for you; other times you will have to identify potential issues based on a set of facts. Either way, an essential component of your research will be developing a list of terms that will define your issue and guide your research. As your research progresses, you will often need to return to this list, to clarify or expand it, until you are confident that you have adequately identified the terms that frame your issue.

The first step in developing a list of terms is to look closely at the facts you have been asked to analyze.[1] Use these facts to generate a list of terms. At the beginning of your research, take a brainstorming approach to generate as many useful terms as possible. Do not rely on search engines to perform this step for you, although they can be helpful starting points. The most sophisticated research algorithms are programmed to search for alternatives, but your research will be more effective if you begin with a thorough list of terms.

---

1. In law school, professors typically provide the universe of facts for an issue. In practice, attorneys and paralegals gather the facts through means such as interviewing clients and witnesses, visiting the scene of an accident or crime, taking depositions, and subpoenaing records.

One method of generating research terms is to ask questions similar to the journalistic approach of who, what, when, where, and why.

1) **Who** are the parties involved in the case? Rather than names, think of identifying characteristics, such as teacher, student, landowner, trespasser, doctor, or patient.

2) **What** are the parties trying to accomplish? Does one of the parties want to be compensated for an injury, or enforce the terms of a contract?

3) **When** did the situation that created the legal issue occur? Although it might be relevant that something occurred at precisely 5:17 p.m., think more generally about what came before the situation, and what followed it.

4) **Where** did the situation arise? Again, look for identifying characteristics of the place where the situation arose, not necessarily the street address. Examples might include a school gym, a rural piece of property, or a hospital.

5) **Why** is the person bringing the legal issue, or why does the defendant think there is no liability? In your early work, you will likely be told the claim or defense by your supervisor. As you gain legal experience, you will begin identifying these for yourself.

Another method of analyzing facts and generating research terms uses a mnemonic device — TARPP — to help with brainstorming. In the TARPP method, you generate a list of relevant Things, Actions, Relief, People, and Places regarding your facts.

It makes little difference which method you use to generate research vocabulary. The point is to analyze the facts and the legal issues and generate terms that will help with research in indexes, tables of contents, topic guides, and other "finding tools," as well as in full-text searching.

After generating an initial research vocabulary, list synonyms and antonyms for each term. This extra step helps to expand the research possibilities and increases the likelihood that you will find results that are on point. You might also think of which terms you wish to exclude from your results, especially in online research. For example, if you are searching the racketeering law known as RICO, you may not want to review documents concerning Puerto Rico.

Novice researchers, or even experienced researchers who are researching a new field, often find legal dictionaries and thesauri helpful in developing research terms that legal sources traditionally use. A legal dictionary, such as *Black's Law Dictionary* (10th ed. 2014), or a legal thesaurus, will help you to develop a broad list of research terms that are likely to appear in other legal sources.[2]

B. Use Secondary Sources for Background Knowledge

Secondary sources, such as treatises, law review articles, and legal encyclopedias, are often used in the early stages of research to help you gain background knowledge of the legal issue. Which secondary sources you use depends on how much you already know about the topic and how broad or narrow the problem is. How many secondary sources you use will depend on how successful your early searches are.[3]

Use the index, table of contents, full-text searching, or other search methods[4] in each secondary authority, working with the research vocabulary you generated earlier. When researching online, conduct multiple searches using different terms in order to find all relevant portions of the secondary authority. When using print sources, thoroughly search the index for all research terms before turning to the text of the secondary authority. You will be less likely to inadvertently omit research terms or duplicate your research.

C. Find Primary Authority

Secondary sources are good tools to help find primary authority because secondary sources often cite directly to primary authority either in text or in footnotes. In addition to reading primary authority referred to in secondary sources, remember to search directly for all three types of primary authority—cases, statutes and constitutional provisions, and administrative regulations. Research tools available both online and in print allow you to search directly for primary authorities through indexes (sometimes called *digests*), by topic, and through full-text searching.

After compiling a list of primary authorities from secondary sources and various finding tools, you must read and analyze each case, constitutional pro-

---

2. A legal dictionary is also essential when you are first starting to read and analyze cases. Some words and phrases non-lawyers use, such as "reckless," have a particular meaning in a legal context; conversely, legal sources still use phrases in indexing, such as "Master and Servant," that are no longer in common use by non-lawyers.

3. For more information on secondary sources, see Chapter 6.

4. These research methods are explained in Chapter 1.

vision, statute, or regulation to determine its impact on your client's situation. In this process, do not disregard primary authority that is negative for the client. A properly prepared attorney must be able to respond to negative primary authority and explain why it does not control the case. Furthermore, an attorney has a professional and ethical duty to inform the court of negative, binding authority that is directly on point.

D. Update

Because the law is constantly changing, attorneys must constantly update their research to adequately represent their clients' interests. A common term for updating is "Shepardizing" because the first major tools for updating were books called *Shepard's Citations*. Now, many online research services have a *citator*, a feature providing a list of subsequent sources that cite the authority being updated. In addition to Shepard's, which is available on Lexis, an updating service called KeyCite is available on Westlaw. By referring to a source like Shepard's or KeyCite, the researcher learns whether subsequent authorities still follow a particular case or whether it has been reversed, overruled, or criticized by later courts.

Updating can be time consuming when done correctly because analyzing relevant sources on the results list requires concentration. But it is also critical for ensuring that the authorities you are relying on are current.[5]

II. When to Stop Researching

At some point, you must decide to stop researching. Often this decision is dictated by deadlines or by the client's resources. In addition, a good researcher knows not to search forever for the one case, statute, or regulation that exactly

---

5. In one situation, a former student of one of the authors who was clerking at a large law firm was asked to respond to a motion to dismiss a complaint. In researching the issues, the clerk quickly discovered that the attorney who wrote the complaint had relied heavily on a case that had been overruled nearly fifteen years earlier. Needless to say, the case was dismissed. Furthermore, the plaintiff's attorneys were ordered to pay the defendant's attorney's fees because the case was frivolous. So, in addition to losing credibility before judges and colleagues, failing to update research can also cost a lawyer money in opposing counsel's fees and legal malpractice claims.

answers the question. This is because legal issues requiring research seldom have clear answers. Often, novice researchers either under- or over-research legal issues. As you gain more experience, you will know when to "call it quits." Until then, here are some helpful hints.

You should not stop researching until you have at least considered all types of primary authority that may be relevant. In addition, you must update every primary authority on which your analysis relies.

In general, focus your research on the jurisdiction where your issue arose. You may find dozens of articles on a particular legal issue, but only a few of them are likely to address developments in your state or circuit. However, if you find you are dealing with an issue of first impression in your jurisdiction, do not stop researching until you know whether other jurisdictions have already resolved the issue.

As a general rule, you can stop researching when the sources you consult are leading back to the same primary authority or rules of law, or when you begin to see the same authorities over and over.

If you follow the research process described here and find nothing on point, consider (1) expanding your research vocabulary, (2) reviewing more secondary sources, and (3) returning to the supervisor for additional guidance.

Finally, do not be afraid to start writing. One of the most time-wasting mistakes made by novice researchers is trying to do "all" of the research before they begin writing. Often attorneys do not find the gaps in their research and, more importantly, their analysis, until they start writing. When your writing reveals such a gap, go back through the steps summarized above and explained in other chapters to fill in those gaps.

III. Varying the Research Process

Sometimes you will begin the research process with a good background understanding of the legal issues involved, or even with a citation to primary authority. In that situation, you might not need to develop a research vocabulary or review secondary sources to begin your research. If you begin your research knowing which statute is relevant, you could use an annotated code to find cases interpreting that statute. If you have a citation to a relevant case, you could begin your work by reading the case and using it as a springboard to other primary authorities — reading the authorities it cites and then updating the case to find later cases that have cited it.

Even when you begin your research with a citation to primary authority, however, it is still a good idea to go through all of the research steps to ensure thorough research. To continue the prior example, if you simply rely on one case and subsequent cases stemming from that one case, you may never find a line of cases or a statute conflicting with the line of cases you researched. Even if you know you want to go directly to primary authority, such as when you are looking for a Florida statutory provision, taking a moment to think about research terms will ensure that you do not stop your research too soon. Similarly, checking for secondary sources discussing that statutory provision, such as periodical articles, may give you a broader understanding of how that provision fits into a larger statutory scheme and help you anticipate additional issues.

Using online research tools and search engines does not eliminate the need to go through the research steps described here. An online search, even using a general search engine such as Google, can be an excellent way to develop research terms or identify starting points for further research in primary authorities. Free or low-cost options for finding cases, such as Google Scholar or Fastcase, can also be a springboard for launching research into an issue that is likely to be controlled by case law. Westlaw and Lexis make it easy to move back and forth between secondary sources, primary sources, and updating tools.

However, whether you gain access to your sources through a print index or through a screen, there is no substitute for the process of generating a list of relevant terms, finding background information, locating controlling authority, and ensuring that the primary sources you are relying on have not been modified or rejected. Whether these steps occur in turn, or whether you move back and forth between the steps as you learn more about your issue, is not really important. What is important is arriving at a conclusion that is well founded and based on the most current law available.

Chapter 1

Planning and Organizing Research

Every research project should begin with a plan for conducting the research and with ideas for organizing research results. Having an effective research plan will increase the reliability of your research results. The plan must include each of the fundamental steps outlined in this book's Introduction, even when research methods vary. As you go through these steps, you will need to record your research methods and organize the authorities that you find. And, in most instances, you will need to turn that raw information into a written work product, or at the very least, into an outline that you can use for an oral discussion of the project. This chapter will discuss each of these areas—planning your research, searching effectively through a variety of research methods, recording and organizing your findings, and using them to create a product. As you gain experience conducting legal research, return to this chapter and implement its suggestions.

I. Planning Your Research

A research plan begins with asking yourself certain threshold questions about the type of issue you are addressing. From there, you choose the specific sources you will consult and the media you will use for each, keeping in mind that sources may be added to your plan (or removed from it) as your research progresses.

A. Asking Threshold Questions

Asking yourself certain initial questions will help you avoid gaps in your research later.

- Does this project present issues of purely state law, purely federal law, or a combination of both? Knowing which law is likely to be involved will determine which sources you will consult.

- Is this primarily a common law issue, statutory issue, or regulatory issue? Note that the answer does not relieve you of the responsibility for checking all three types of authority, but may guide your starting point.

- When did your issue arise? If the applicable law has changed, you will need to be especially clear about dates so that you can focus your research on the law that was in effect at the time.

- Is this a rapidly evolving area of the law or a more established area? Your answer may determine which secondary sources will be the most helpful.

- What limitations do you have, whether practical or analytical? Cost and time are obvious limitations that can affect your choice of sources and media. You may be asked to analyze only one aspect of an issue, while other lawyers work on other aspects; keeping that clearly in mind will help you focus on your goal.

B. Choosing Sources

The considerations to keep in mind when choosing sources are covered in more detail in the chapters devoted to those sources. For purposes of developing a research plan, what is important is that you consciously choose sources that best suit your research project, rather than always starting with a particular source.

When beginning with a project in an unfamiliar area of law, visit secondary sources early on. These sources can save you time, money, and most importantly, the chagrin of missing an important aspect of your issue. As noted in the Introduction, secondary sources can provide context, help you identify whether various jurisdictions approach your issue similarly, and point to citations to primary authority.

Which secondary source you use depends on the project. If the legal area is well established and you need general background information, an encyclopedia or treatise may be a good beginning point. If the legal area is relatively new, law review articles or Continuing Legal Education (CLE) materials may offer the only treatment available in secondary sources.

If you are researching an area that you know from past work, or if a supervisor gives you a relevant case or statute to begin your research, beginning your research plan with primary authority makes sense. For all primary authority, tools exist that allow you to find lists of cases that have cited that authority. Annotated statutes, for example, provide not only the text of each statute, but also lists of cases that cite that statute. Citators can also lead quickly to additional relevant authority, including secondary sources that address the issue.

In planning research in general, remember that answering a question often requires looking at more than one type of primary authority. This is most evident when doing statutory research, where you must look for regulations that provide important detail to the statutory scheme and you must locate cases interpreting the relevant statute. Thus, be sure that in designing every research plan you consider the possible existence of relevant statutes and constitutional provisions, case law, and administrative materials.

Every research plan must also include updating the primary sources on which your legal analysis relies. Updating typically means using either the Shepard's service on Lexis or Westlaw's KeyCite service to determine whether these primary authorities have received negative treatment or whether they are still "good law."

In a broader sense, however, updating means researching thoroughly enough to present a current and accurate view of the law. One example of insufficient updating would be verifying that a statute has not been modified recently, using legislative materials, without doing case law research to learn whether a court has ever called the constitutionality of the statute into question. Another example would be verifying that an older case describing a common law doctrine has not been overruled, and then relying exclusively on that case, without reading enough newer cases to determine whether the language in the earlier case is consistent with the current approach or determining whether the common law rule has been integrated into a statutory scheme.

C. Choosing Media

The choice to use print or online sources, just like other choices described earlier, should be a conscious one. If you develop the habit of always logging onto Westlaw as soon as you get a research assignment, you are short-changing your research process just as surely as you would if you always started by looking for statutes or by reading a legal encyclopedia.[1]

---

1. Each of these automatic decisions could result in inefficient research: another tool might provide material not available on Westlaw (e.g., an older law review article), a project might be controlled by common law (meaning your statutory search was bound to fail), and an encyclopedia would be an unlikely source for finding information about emerging legal issues.

Many attorneys find that beginning research in print is more helpful when working in an unfamiliar area of law. Even after mastering a certain area of law, many attorneys find that quickly turning to a *deskbook* (a book devoted to one legal practice area) in print can be a productive way to launch their online research.

Online research is typically more effective when you have a definite starting point (e.g., a citation to a relevant case or other authority) or when researching narrow areas of law (e.g., researching a particular tort may be more efficient online than researching a rule of civil procedure). Westlaw and Lexis still enjoy some advantages over most Internet sites, including constant updating, sophisticated search mechanisms, cross-referencing among the sources, and the existence of specialized topical databases. Bloomberg is a relatively new online provider, but it has sophisticated search tools and is especially effective when you are researching in areas of business law or when you need court documents. Fastcase is a more modest online service, but it is free to members of The Florida Bar. Table 1-1 summarizes the more common online services.

The Internet is often an excellent source for current state and federal legislative information. Tracking bills that have recently been introduced in the Florida Legislature, for example, can easily be done on the state legislature websites. Administrative agencies are providing most of their material on Internet sites as well. While the Internet can be a helpful springboard for your research, remember to look at each site critically. Official government sites, and those of university or state libraries, are usually regarded as highly reliable. Even when using one of these sites, however, it is possible that you will follow a link that takes you to a less reliable or less frequently updated source. This puts a heavier burden on you to evaluate the reliability of information. Always check to see when the site you are using was last updated, and by whom. Table 1-2 contains addresses for a number of reliable sites.

Table 1-1. Online Providers for Legal Research

Name	Status	Coverage	Citator	Notes
Bloomberg	Premium	Extensive coverage of cases, statutes, and regulations, with emphasis on linking legal and financial information; provides access to federal court dockets; highly regarded for specific practice areas such as intellectual property, employee benefits, and banking	BCite	
Casemaker	Low-Cost	State and federal case law, state and federal statutes, a limited number of administrative materials and secondary sources	CASEcheck	Free to members of some state bar associations
Fastcase	Low-Cost	State and federal case law, statutory law, regulations, and court rules	Authority Check	Free to members of The Florida Bar
Google Scholar	Free	Cases and scholarly articles	How cited	No statutory or regulatory laws are included
Lexis Advance	Premium	Extensive state, national, and international material, extensive secondary sources	Shepard's	
Loislaw	Low-Cost	Extensive state and federal databases, as well as a library of treatises	GlobalCite	
VersusLaw	Low-Cost	State and federal appellate court decisions, some federal trial court decisions, and federal statutes and regulations; has a collection of tribal law decisions	V.Cite	
Westlaw Classic	Premium	Extensive state, national, and international material, extensive secondary sources	KeyCite	Still available in practice, but not in academia
WestlawNext	Premium	Extensive state, national, and international material, extensive secondary sources	KeyCite	

Table 1-2. Research Bookmarks

Bookmarking reliable legal research sites can speed your research. Suggested bookmarks are listed below. Organizing your bookmarks into folders, such as "Florida Statutes," "Florida Cases," "Federal Research," and relevant topical folders, will help you locate information more quickly. Folders can easily be added for specific research projects.

Florida Links

Florida Courts	www.flcourts.org
Online Sunshine	www.leg.state.fl.us
The Florida Bar	www.floridabar.org

Compilations of Legal Links

ALSO! (American Law Sources Online)	www.lawsource.com/also
FindLaw	www.findlaw.com
Government Information Resources	http://guides.lib.virginia.edu/findinggovinfo
Cornell's Legal Information Institute	www.law.cornell.edu
PublicLegal (Internet Legal Research Group)	www.ilrg.com

Gateways to Federal Research Links and Information

Congressional Research Reports	www.opencrs.com
GPO* Federal Digital System	www.gpo.gov/fdsys
Government Accountability Office	www.gao.gov
Congress.gov	http://beta.congress.gov

Multi-Jurisdictional State Law Research

Council of State Governments	www.csg.org
Municipal Code Corporation	www.municode.com
National Center for State Courts	www.ncsconline.org
National Conference of State Legislatures	www.ncsl.org
National Health Information Center	www.health.gov/nhic
State and Local Government on the Net	www.statelocalgov.net
Uniform Law Commission	www.uniformlaws.org

U.S. Supreme Court Research

Supreme Court of the United States	www.supremecourt.gov
Supreme Court Center (FindLaw)	http://supreme.lp.findlaw.com
U.S. Supreme Court Media	www.oyez.org

* GPO Access is published by the Government Printing Office, which will soon be called the Government Publishing Office. The GPO Access site is migrating to a new site called Congress.gov.

II. Using Varied Research Methods

In designing your research plan, consider which research methods are most likely to be effective for your current project. The many research tools you encounter when doing legal research will allow you to conduct research using a variety of methods, ranging from a simple review of an index or a single-word search in the full text of documents to a complex search with sophisticated terms and connectors. The keys are to know which services, sites, or books are most likely to contain the resources you need and how to search them effectively. This part of the chapter highlights a few of the more popular search techniques. For specific information, visit a website's "Help" or "Tips" link or review the introductory material of a book.[2]

A. Index Searching

An index lists in alphabetical order the terms that describe important concepts included in any set of resources, whether sections of a statutory code or chapters of a treatise. Online, you will likely see just the most general terms on the first screen of an index. Clicking on each term or on an icon next to it will often expand the list to more specific terms. When you find the most relevant terms, you will be led to documents discussing those terms or to a portion of the document with text on that concept. In print, indexes typically appear in the first or last volume of multi-volume series, or at the back of a single volume. Print indexes can refer researchers to particular pages, paragraphs, sections, or chapters where the topic is covered.

B. Table of Contents Searching

A table of contents lists the major topics of a work in the order in which they appear in the work. Thus, a table of contents for a treatise will provide the names of chapters and sections of the treatise. A table of contents for a statutory code will list the titles and subtitles of statutes in numerical order. Reviewing a table of contents has one benefit over reviewing an index: you will see topics in context, advancing your understanding of that area of law.

---

2. Chapter 2, Part III.A., of this book explains methods for researching cases online; those methods are generally applicable to online searching, so you may want to review that section when learning to search for statutes, regulations, secondary sources, etc.

C. Topic Searching

Topic searching takes place on both a macro and a micro level. On the macro level, certain services, sites, and books are devoted to single topics, or even to specific areas of those topics. Looking at a service or website devoted to criminal law, or even to the specific crime of homicide, will likely be more effective than reviewing all of a service's content or searching on a website with general coverage. On the micro level, a number of online services provide topical outlines that work somewhat like tables of contents. You begin to use one of these outlines by clicking on a link such as "Browse Topics." On Lexis Advance, for example, topics range from Banking Law, to Family Law, to Trademark Law. After you select one of the broad topics, you can narrow your search to a specific sub-topic. The search results will all be focused on the topics and sub-topics you select.

D. Natural Language Searching

Natural language searching is the term some legal services use for what is commonly called "Googling." You type in a word, a string of words, or a question related to the issue you are researching, and the search engine retrieves related documents. For example, searching "proof of homicide" from the universal search bar of Lexis Advance or WestlawNext could retrieve secondary sources, statutes, pending legislation, and cases on that topic.

E. Terms and Connectors Searching

The most controlled way to search is using terms and connectors. Inserting connectors and commands into a search allows you to require that the terms appear within a certain proximity, and even in a certain order. To create a terms and connectors search, select from your research vocabulary those terms most likely to appear in the documents you seek. Modify the terms to allow the search engine to find alternative spellings (e.g., use dr*nk to find drink, drank, or drunk) or endings (e.g., use communicat! to find communication, communications, communicated, etc.). Combine your terms using connectors unique to the website you are searching, noting that some are contradictory (e.g., a space between two terms could create a phrase like *summary judgment* or it could tell the service to search for documents containing either "summary" or "judgment"). While creating a terms and connectors search takes a bit of effort, it puts the researcher in charge of the search; in contrast, running a natural language search is easier, but it lets the search engine create the search.

III. Organizing the Research

One of the most challenging components of legal research is keeping the research organized. Organization is especially troublesome to novice researchers, though it can plague even an experienced lawyer who is researching a complex legal issue. Developing good organizational skills is crucial. Being organized saves research time because it keeps you from inadvertently repeating steps of the research process. Moreover, good research organization produces more thorough legal analysis because it encourages critical thinking while the research progresses. Being organized also saves time in the writing process because the authority supporting each analytical point is easier to locate when you need it.

There are many ways to organize research. Which method you use is not as important as developing a method of organizing research that works for you. At a minimum, begin with a research plan and take notes while you are researching. For a more complicated research project, consider developing an outline as you do your research.

A. Research Notes

Write out your research plan, beginning with the threshold questions in Part I.A. of this chapter. Then decide which secondary and primary sources you intend to research, and in which order. For each source, consider which media you prefer from those that are available to you. Then decide which methods you will use to conduct your research. Writing out your plan should take just a few minutes, but the systematic approach should ensure highly reliable results.

As you work through your research plan, keep notes of your progress. You certainly want to take advantage of the "History" links when online services provide them. But your research notes need to be more comprehensive than those links allow because you are likely going to use multiple sources in commercial services, governmental websites, and books. Table 1-3 provides hints for taking notes effectively.

Table 1-3. Hints for Effective Note-Taking

1. Be specific in listing the sources you have checked. Which books, websites, or online services did you use?

2. For each source, list the exact words and combinations of words that you used in searching the index, table of contents, or full text. Note whether you used "Browse Topics" or searched a database restricted to Florida state cases.

3. The content or results that you record from each source will depend on the source you are researching. For case research, you may want to record the following information for each relevant case: facts, issues, quotable passages, the court's holding, page numbers for critical analysis in the opinion, and all citation information.

4. Try to use each source as a finding tool for additional research. Secondary sources include both commentary and footnotes to other secondary and primary authority. Court decisions contain citations to previous cases that may also be on point. Annotated statutes will list cross references to secondary sources and cases.

Your research notes should include at least the following information: (1) the sources you have checked; (2) the topics, words, issues, and index terms you researched in each source; (3) the results (or content) of the research you found in each source; (4) additional sources you may want to look up based on the sources you have already checked; and (5) updates for each source. The time you spend making these notes will be recouped in several ways. You will be able to put your research aside and return to it—a common occurrence in law practice—without having to retrace your steps. If you recognize a new or additional issue during your research, you will be in a better position to recognize which sources will lead you to authority addressing that issue. And, during the writing process, you will be able to insert citations as you draft, rather than having to rediscover where you found a particular bit of information.

B. Online Folders and Tabs

Legal research often produces many documents that you must skim to decide whether they are relevant, and you need a system to help you keep track of them. For instance, will you read each document as you come to it or compile a list of multiple documents to read later? If you are researching in print, it is common to have multiple books open on your desk at the same time. Using "post-it notes" and piling books in related stacks can help you keep track.

If you are researching online, you can open multiple documents on your virtual desktop. Using the electronic folders and tabs provided by various services can help you stay organized. To begin, create a new folder for this research project. On Lexis Advance, do this from the link "My Workspace." From WestlawNext, click on the "Folders" link. As you conduct your research, save relevant searches and documents to this folder by clicking on the icon of a folder with an arrow. In addition to keeping organized, you will save money as Lexis Advance and WestlawNext do not charge you for re-reading documents in folders. (Also consider creating a sub-folder where you will put discarded cases; you don't want to delete them from a folder altogether or you might end up paying to read the documents again.) Additional advantages to creating folders are the ability to share them with colleagues who are working on the same project and the opportunity to download them so that you can work without an Internet connection.

The next hurdle is deciding which documents are relevant and deserve to be in a folder. The following two options are listed simply to show you alternatives. You will find out quickly whether one of these options is efficient for you, or you might develop another alternative.

(1) *Open each possibly relevant document in a new tab to read later.* For example, while reading a relevant section of a treatise, click on each case, statute, or other source that seems interesting, but immediately go back to the treatise until you have completed reading that one section. This approach will allow you to maintain concentration on the key concepts without being distracted by the facts of a particular case or the details of a possibly related statute. When you have finished reading that section of the treatise, open each of the tabs and read the documents. Save any relevant documents to a folder.

(2) *Skim each document quickly as you encounter it.* Continuing with the treatise example, decide immediately whether each document you encounter deserves a closer reading, and if so put it in your folder. The benefit of this approach is that you initially read each document as you encounter it in the treatise and know the point of law that it should discuss. The downside is that you lose the context of the treatise.

Frequently in your research — perhaps every few hours — read carefully the new documents you have added to your folder. Decide whether to keep them there or to move them to a sub-folder of discarded documents. Use the service's annotation feature to highlight or add notes to each document.

As you determine which documents are the most important, consider the format in which you will read them most thoroughly. For some researchers, reading key documents in print is still the most effective way to achieve deep understanding. Other researchers find that reading on a large computer screen is just as effective as reading in print; using multiple screens allows shifting easily between documents without wasting time or losing context. However, reading legal documents on a small pad or phone is unlikely to lead to full understanding because of the tendency to skim text quickly and the lack of context. If you read documents on your computer, consider closing programs, websites, or apps that might distract you as you read.

C. Research Outlines

A research outline can be a bridge from research to writing. Some legal researchers prefer to save the outlining stage for when they actually begin drafting a brief or other document. However, some researchers find it very helpful to organize their research notes into an outline even before they begin drafting.

To create a research outline, you will need to do enough background reading to identify the likely issues and sub-issues that may arise in your research project. For example, assume you are analyzing the effect of a contract between an employer and employee. The contract restricts the employee's ability to work in the same industry or profession after the employee leaves the employer. Some preliminary reading in a basic employment law treatise or a legal encyclopedia will reveal that these are called "covenants not to compete" and that they are governed by statute.[3] Reading the statute, in turn, reveals several terms that you will have to analyze on a case-by-case basis in lawsuits involving covenants not to compete: the restriction must be reasonable, and the employer seeking to enforce the restriction must prove that legitimate business interests support the restriction. You realize that you will need to find, among other sources, cases that have analyzed whether a specific restriction was (a) reasonable or (b) supported by legitimate business interests. Those two legal principles might become the main headings in a research outline.

The statute in question further specifies that restrictions must be reasonable in "time, area, and line of business." These might become sub-headings in your outline under "reasonableness." As you read cases, you will take notes on each

---

3. See section 542.335, *Florida Statutes*, for the full statutory provision. The statute includes other requirements not discussed here, such as the requirement of a signed writing.

case, but will put those notes directly into the outline under the sub-heading or sub-headings where the case is most helpful. A case that decided a restriction was unreasonable as to time, for example, and thus did not discuss other provisions of the statute, would appear in only one place on your outline. A case that discusses all three sub-issues will appear three times on your outline. See Table 1-4.

Table 1-4. Preliminary Analysis in a Research Outline

§ 542.335, Fla. Stat.

    (a) reasonableness

        1. reasonable time: Case A, Case B

        2. reasonable area: Case A, Case C

        3. reasonable line of business: Case A, Case B, Case D

    (b) supported by legitimate business interests: Case A, Case C, Case E

An advantage of using the outlining method for note-taking is that gaps in your research are easy to identify. Of course, there are other ways to accomplish this. Even if you simply take notes on sources in the order in which you consult them, you can make margin notes to remind yourself which issues or sub-issues each source addresses.

D. A Research Notebook

Although the precise method of organizing research is a matter of personal preference, the following explains in some detail one effective method of organizing a research project. When you have finished researching using the research notebook method described below, you will have a list of all sources you have checked, a list of all primary authority found, a summary sheet for each relevant case, a list of Shepard's or KeyCite results, and a complete outline with primary authorities supporting each point.

The research notebook method was developed by an attorney who preferred to have key documents in print.[4] Following her approach, you would need a binder that has removable pages and five dividers labeled: Sources, Primary

---

4. This portion of the chapter is based on material in the first edition of *Florida Legal Research* that was written by co-author Lisa Kuhlman Tietig.

Authority, Summaries, Updating, and Outline. You could keep similar notes on your computer, creating five folders with the headings listed above.

1. List of Sources and Terms

As you are researching, keep a separate list of all the sources you have checked. For example, include the names of articles you have read and the names of online providers whose content you searched. For each source, list the research terms or topics checked within each source. Note the search method that you used (e.g., full-text searching, browsing topics). As your research progresses, add to your research vocabulary any new terms that you learn that may lead to relevant authority, remembering that different sources may index helpful material under different terms.

This list of sources and terms serves three purposes: (1) to keep you from duplicating research; (2) to help you remember what topics or terms were helpful so that you can check those topics or terms in other sources; and (3) to help stir ideas for new topics to examine.

2. List of Primary Authority

Keep a separate section in your notebook, or a separate online file, that lists all of the cases, statutes, and regulations you have found. This list helps prevent duplicating research. You will often find references to a relevant authority in several sources. As you read the authority, mark on your list whether the authority is on point, as noted below. Then when another source refers to the same authority, you will readily know you have already reviewed it.

If you later discard a case, cross the case off your list of primary authorities with one line so that you will not go back to the case later. Be sure that the case name and citation are still legible when you cross the case off your list. If you are keeping notes on your computer either have a separate file for "Discarded Authority" or use the "Reviewing" toolbar to strike out, but not to delete, unneeded cases.

In the back of this section of your notebook, you may also want to include copies of the cases, statutes, and regulations you intend to cite in writing your document.

3. Case Summary Sheets

Although statutes and regulations are just as important as case law, researchers usually have far more cases in their list of primary authority than they do statutes or regulations. The reason is that, even when only one or two statutes or regulations apply to the client's problem, there may be many cases interpreting those few statutes and regulations. For this reason, organization methods specific to case law are helpful. Some of these methods are explained next.

a. Read Groups of Cases

Reading cases in groups will, ultimately, save you time and enhance your understanding of the issue. A good default option is reading cases in chronological order. This approach will help you see the development of the law and identify leading cases, statutes, or regulations. It will also help to solidify your understanding of the client's issue and help you determine which cases are most relevant. If you have reason to anticipate recent developments in the area you are researching, or if your group of cases includes very recent decisions from the highest court in your jurisdiction, you might choose to read them in reverse chronological order. This approach will still help you see the development of the law over time.

Another option, when reading cases decided by Florida state courts, is to begin with cases from the Florida Supreme Court, then to read cases decided by each district court of appeal, beginning with the district in which your issue arises. This grouping is especially important if your research reveals conflict among the five districts. If your research issue arose in the Third District, you do not want to read a long line of cases from the First District Court of Appeal only to realize that those cases will not be helpful to you because of a conflict.

b. Information Included in a Case Summary Sheet

Taking careful notes on relevant cases is critical. Many attorneys call these "case briefs," but that term can be confusing. While a case brief might address all of the legal points in a case, a case summary sheet includes only information that is important for solving the current client's issue. Writing case summary sheets ensures that you have carefully read each relevant case and decided how the case affects your client's issue. Creating a case summary sheet for each case ensures that your case law research is well organized when you are ready to begin writing. And reviewing a short stack of case summary sheets is much easier than reviewing each case whenever you need support for a key idea.

A sample case summary sheet is included in the appendix to this chapter, along with an excerpt of the case as annotated on WestlawNext. Be sure to include each piece of information necessary for correct citation, such as the jurisdiction and the date.

Under the citation, list the relevant headnotes from that case. Headnotes are short summaries of the key points in a case. They appear before the opinion and serve as a table of contents for a case. Each has a sequential number (e.g., HN3). When you update the case with Shepard's or KeyCite, you will give special note to subsequent sources that have cited the case for those headnotes. If the case seems very important, or directly on point, then you may want to read all the authorities listed as citing sources.

Read the case carefully once again. Identify the portion of the case that is on point, and highlight important points or quotes. In the margin, number each underlined portion of the case. When you are finished reading the case, go back to each numbered point in the case and make a note of the significant point on the case summary sheet. The number of the note on your case summary sheet should correspond to the number you wrote in the margin of the case. Next to each note on the case summary sheet, in the left-hand margin, list the page number of the case where the information was found. This will give you the pinpoint citation when you are ready to write. It can also be helpful if you are working with a lengthy decision and need to re-read portions of the decision later.

4. Updating List[5]

As discussed in Chapter 5, updating should take place at least twice for each primary authority you rely on: (1) early in your research, to verify that the authority has not been overruled or abrogated and to find additional relevant authorities; and (2) just before submitting your document, to ensure that no authority has been undermined while you were working on your project. Keeping track of the different points of updating requires organization. Either on your list of primary authorities or on each document itself, include a quick note that indicates you checked Shepard's or KeyCite to be sure that the authority is still respected. (Remember that you can annotate cases in your folders on Lexis Advance and WestlawNext.) In addition, keep a list of cases you encounter as you update, noting new cases that seem to be on point (including cases that you do not find helpful will keep you from re-reading them). These cases might expand your research universe if the analysis is particularly clear or if the facts are closer to your client's situation. Just before you submit a document, check one final time to ensure that nothing has happened during the days or weeks that you were working on a project.

---

5. Regardless of which tools you use for updating, you must update each authority you rely on for your analysis. An attorney has an obligation to the client and to the court to update research, as explained in Chapter 5. *See Glassalum Eng'g Corp. v. 392208 Ontario Ltd.*, 487 So. 2d 87, 88 (Fla. 3d DCA 1986).

Also remember to update statutes and regulations. Focus on the specific part of the statute or regulation that is relevant to your work. Otherwise, you could read many citing cases that are not on point because they refer to a portion of the statute or regulation that is not pertinent for your work. At the top of each statute or regulation (or on your list of primary authorities), make a notation of the date when you updated the authority. When you do your final updating before submitting your document, you will know how much further updating is needed.

5. Research Outline

As soon as you recognize the structure of your legal issue, create an outline as described in section III.C., above.

IV. Turning Research into a Work Product

At the beginning of every project, you should have a target date for when you will begin to write (or prepare your oral report) based on the due date of that project. Stick to that target date; don't let the research process become an excuse for procrastinating.

Your research should reveal the main points of an analytical outline. List those outline points in the proper hierarchy. Then go through your primary authorities and list each authority next to the points on the outline that the authority supports. (This is the fifth step in creating a research notebook, discussed above.)

At the end of that process, if you have points in your outline with no corresponding primary authority, you have identified a gap to fill through additional research. Continue alternating between researching and outlining until you have identified authority that will allow you to support your analysis of each point on the outline.

Some people do not find detailed outlining helpful. If you have checked all of the sources you identified in your research plan and updated each primary authority you located, you are probably ready to begin writing a rough draft of your document. You might try a "pre-writing" strategy to get started, such as giving yourself a set amount of time (10–15 minutes) to simply write about your research results without stopping to look at your sources. Or you might try creating a diagram of the different issues and sub-issues your research has identified.

Do not worry if, after you have started to write, you find a point for which you need additional authority; writing and researching are not completely distinct processes. Even if you have sufficient authority, the writing process may help you refine your thoughts in a way that allows you to see other authorities in a different light. Circling back and forth between writing and research is normal.

Appendix: Case Summary Sheet and Annotated Case

This case summary sheet contains the following information about *Broudy v. Broudy*:

1) The correct citation;
2) The relevant headnotes (if you find a large number of citing cases when you update *Broudy*, you should focus on those cases that refer to headnotes 8 or 9);
3) The points in the case that are relevant to your issue and the pages in the case where those points are discussed.

Sample Case Summary Sheet

Broudy v. Broudy,
423 So. 2d 504 (Fla. 3d DCA 1982).

headnotes 8, 9

    p.507   1. Purpose of awarding attorney's fees is to ensure both parties are able to secure competent legal counsel.

    p.508   2. In dissolution of marriage enforcement action, party's unwillingness to comply with marital settlement agreement justified award of attorney's fees to party seeking enforcement.

Sample Annotated Case

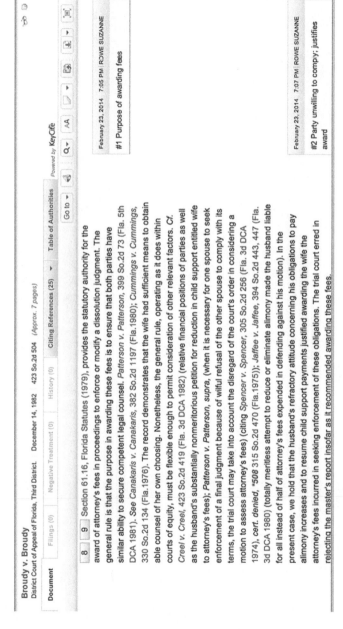

Source: WestlawNext. Reprinted with permission of Thomson Reuters.

Chapter 2

Judicial Decisions

Analyzing cases is one of the first skills taught in law school, with good reason. Our system of law depends on judicial decision-making. Whether a particular rule is created through legislation or through the common law, a court will eventually be called upon to apply the rule to resolve a dispute between two or more parties. Understanding how courts have decided similar legal issues in the past allows an attorney to counsel a client about how the rule is likely to be applied in the client's case, as well as to advocate for that client if a dispute arises.

The weight to be given to a particular case depends, in part, on which court decided that case. Therefore, this chapter begins with an overview of the Florida and federal court systems. Then it explains *reporters*, the books containing published court decisions. Because decisions are still typically cited to reporters, being familiar with reporters is important even when conducting research online. Next this chapter explains a variety of methods for finding cases, with a focus on Florida law. The chapter ends with a discussion of case analysis.

I. Court Systems

A. Florida State Courts[1]

Like most states, Florida has trial courts (called "circuit courts" or "county courts"), intermediate appellate courts (called "district courts of appeal" and often referred to as "DCAs"), and a court of final appeals (called the "supreme court"). In some situations, the circuit courts also serve as appellate courts for the county courts. Each circuit and county court is within a particular appellate district, as shown in Figure 2-1.

---

1. Further information about the Florida court system, including links to individual court websites and court rules, can be found at www.flcourts.org.

Florida is divided into five appellate districts. The district courts of appeal have both mandatory and discretionary authority, depending on the type of decision being appealed. In other words, the district courts must hear certain appeals, but can decline to hear others. For the vast majority of litigants in Florida, the district courts of appeal are the courts of last resort.

Figure 2-1. Florida's Appellate Districts*

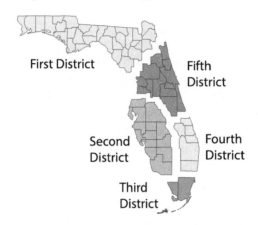

* The First District extends from Pensacola to Jacksonville, including Tallahassee and Gainesville. The Second District includes the Tampa, St. Petersburg, and Ft. Myers area. The Third District is principally the Miami area plus the Florida Keys. The Fourth District follows the east coast of Florida from Fort Lauderdale to Indian River County. The Fifth District includes Orlando and Daytona Beach.

Source: Florida Courts, http://flcourts.org/florida-courts/district-court-appeal.stml.

The Florida Supreme Court also has both mandatory and discretionary jurisdiction. Two examples of cases involving the Florida Supreme Court's mandatory jurisdiction are death sentences and decisions declaring state statutes or constitutional provisions invalid. When a party has a right to appeal, as in these cases, the appealing party is the *appellant* and the opposing party is the *appellee*. Other matters within the high court's jurisdiction are heard on a discretionary basis. These include cases where two or more of the district courts of appeal are in conflict on a given issue and cases involving "questions of great public importance." In these cases, the party requesting review is the *petitioner* and the opposing party is the *respondent*.[2]

---

2. An essential reference for understanding Florida appellate jurisdiction, as well as other appellate topics, is Philip J. Padovano, *Florida Appellate Practice* (2014 ed.).

Decisions of the Florida Supreme Court are binding on all other Florida courts through the principle of *stare decisis*. Stare decisis means "to stand by things decided."[3] Part of the virtue of a common law system is its predictability; courts should decide similar matters as they have done in the past unless there are significant policy reasons for a change or the legislature has enacted a statute changing the law.

Stare decisis applies only to courts within a specific jurisdiction. Thus, decisions of the Georgia Supreme Court are not authoritative for Florida courts addressing the same legal question. Although the Georgia decisions may be persuasive, they do not determine the outcome of Florida cases.

Under the principle of stare decisis, each court must follow its own prior decisions as well as the decisions of higher appellate courts that may review its decisions. Thus, because Leon County is in the First District, a Leon County judge must follow decisions of the First District Court of Appeal as well as decisions of the Florida Supreme Court. If the First District has not ruled on an issue, but one or more of the other district courts of appeal have, and there is no conflict between those districts, then the trial court in Leon County will be bound by the decision of another district court of appeal.[4] If the First District has ruled on an issue, decisions of the other four district courts of appeal would be only persuasive authority.

B. Federal Courts

The federal system also has trial courts (called "district courts"), appellate courts (called "courts of appeals"), and a court of final appeals (called the "supreme court"). Note that while a Florida appellate court is called a "district court of appeal," in the federal system the "district court" is the trial court. Table 2-1 compares the names of courts in the Florida and federal systems.

Florida is divided into three federal districts: the Northern District of Florida, the Middle District of Florida, and the Southern District of Florida. Florida is in the Eleventh Circuit, along with Georgia and Alabama. Decisions of federal trial courts in these three states are appealed to the Eleventh Circuit. Figure 2-2 has a map of the federal circuits and districts.

In the federal court system, decisions of each of the circuit courts of appeals are binding only on trial courts located within those circuits. In contrast to Florida, where one appellate court can bind trial courts in other districts if

---

3. *Black's Law Dictionary* 1537 (10th ed. 2014).
4. *See State v. Hayes*, 333 So. 2d 51, 52 (Fla. 4th DCA 1976).

Table 2-1. Florida and Federal Court Names

Level of Court	Florida	Federal
Highest Court	Florida Supreme Court	United States Supreme Court
Intermediate Appellate Courts	District Courts of Appeal	Circuit Courts of Appeals
Trial Courts	Circuit Courts County Courts	United States District Courts

those districts have not yet ruled on an issue, the federal appellate courts cannot bind federal trial courts in other circuits.[5]

To decide whether to begin researching state or federal cases, or both, consider the issue involved. As a general principle, matters not specifically enumerated in the U.S. Constitution as being within the control of the federal government fall under the jurisdiction of the states. Tort law and family law are examples of areas traditionally left to the states, while interstate commerce is designated in the Constitution as being a matter for the federal government. There is some overlap in jurisdiction. Both state and federal laws address various environmental law issues. Federal constitutional law issues can appear in traditionally state-regulated areas, such as family law. Sometimes the question of what law is to be applied in a particular situation will be the issue you need to resolve.

When reading federal court decisions, pay careful attention to whether the court is applying federal or state law. Sometimes a case is before a federal court because the parties are from different states.[6] In deciding these *diversity* cases, federal courts are supposed to apply the substantive law of the applicable state—which is sometimes, but not always, the state where the case was filed.[7] Diversity

---

5. *See Hart v. Massanari*, 266 F.3d 1155, 1172–73 (9th Cir. 2001) (explaining why decisions of one circuit court are not binding on the other circuit courts in the federal system).

6. *See* 28 U.S.C. § 1332.

7. *See Erie R.R. Co. v. Tompkins*, 304 U.S. 64 (1938). In Florida and other states, if the law of the state is unclear, the federal court may certify a question to the highest court of the state, requesting guidance. *See, e.g.,* Art. V, § 3(b)(6), Fla. Const.; § 25.031, Fla. Stat. (2013) (allowing the Florida Supreme Court to decide certified questions from the United States Supreme Court or one of the Circuit Courts of Appeals); Fla. R. App. P. 9.150; *see also Clay v. Sun Ins. Office Ltd.*, 363 U.S. 207, 212 (1960) (noting favorably Florida's certification statute); *Lehman Bros. v. Schein*, 416 U.S. 386, 391–92

Figure 2-2. Federal Circuits and Districts

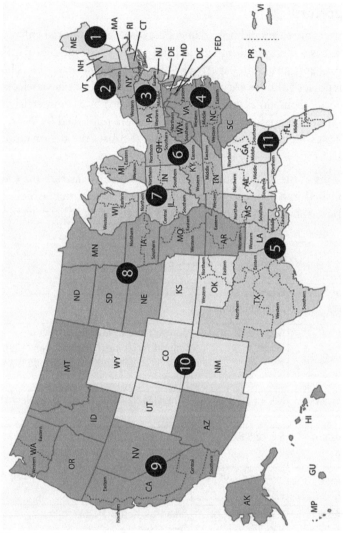

Source: U.S. Courts, http://www.uscourts.gov/uscourts/images/CircuitMap.pdf.

cases may be used in doing state research, although these federal cases are merely persuasive, not binding, on state courts. Always be sure that the court in a diversity case is applying the law of the state you are researching.

(1974) (remanding to Second Circuit to consider certifying question to Florida Supreme Court when applicable Florida law was unsettled).

II. Reporters and Digests

A. Reporters

Reporters are series of books that collect cases, add editorial enhancements, index the cases, and publish them in (more or less) chronological order. Typically, cases appear first in paperback volumes called *advance sheets* before the bound reporter volumes are published. Most jurisdictions have selected an official reporter. Sometimes this is a reporter published by a commercial publisher, but not always. A majority of print reporters are published by West. Table 2-2 lists West's regional reporters, and Table 2-3 lists the major reporters for federal cases.

Opinions of the Florida Supreme Court and the five district courts of appeal are published in a reporter series called *Southern Reporter*, which is a West publication. It has been the official reporter for Florida judicial decisions since

Table 2-2. West's Regional Reporters

Regional Reporters	Citation Abbreviations	State Cases Included
Atlantic Reporter	A. or A.2d	Connecticut, Delaware, District of Columbia, Maine, Maryland, New Hampshire, New Jersey, Pennsylvania, Rhode Island, Vermont
North Eastern Reporter	N.E. or N.E.2d	Illinois, Indiana, Massachusetts, New York, Ohio
South Eastern Reporter	S.E. or S.E.2d	Georgia, North Carolina, South Carolina, Virginia, West Virginia
Southern Reporter	So., So. 2d, or So. 3d	Alabama, Florida, Louisiana, Mississippi
South Western Reporter	S.W., S.W.2d, or S.W.3d	Arkansas, Kentucky, Missouri, Tennessee, Texas
North Western Reporter	N.W. or N.W.2d	Iowa, Michigan, Minnesota, Nebraska, North Dakota, South Dakota, Wisconsin
Pacific Reporter	P., P.2d, or P.3d	Alaska, Arizona, California, Colorado, Hawaii, Idaho, Kansas, Montana, Nevada, New Mexico, Oklahoma, Oregon, Utah, Washington, Wyoming

Table 2-3. Selected Federal Reporters

Reporter	Citation Abbreviation	Court Reported	Publisher
United States Reports*	U.S.	U.S. Supreme Court	U.S. Supreme Court
Supreme Court Reporter	S. Ct.	U.S. Supreme Court	West
United States Supreme Court Reports, Lawyers' Edition	L. Ed. or L. Ed. 2d	U.S. Supreme Court	Lexis
Federal Reporter	F., F.2d, or F.3d	U.S. Courts of Appeals	West
Federal Appendix**	Fed. Appx.	U.S. Courts of Appeals (unpublished decisions)	West
Federal Supplement	F. Supp. or F. Supp. 2d	U.S. District Courts	West

* Citation to the official reporter, *United States Reports*, is required whenever possible; even if you use the *Supreme Court Reporter* or *Lawyers' Edition* for your research, you will have to cite to *United States Reports* if possible. Because *United States Reports* volumes are published more slowly than the other two, however, for recent cases you may have to cite to one of the other reporters.

** Because opinions published in *Federal Appendix* (as well as other unpublished decisions available only online) may be of limited precedential value, it's important to check the rules of the relevant court.

1948. The *Southern Reporter* is a *regional reporter*: it includes cases from the state appellate courts of Florida, Alabama, Louisiana, and Mississippi.

The *Southern Reporter* is currently in its third series. This is referred to as *Southern Reporter, Third* and abbreviated as So. 3d. Cases decided from 1941 to early 2008 were published in the *Southern Reporter, Second*, which is abbreviated as So. 2d. A citation to a case includes the volume, the reporter abbreviation, and the first page of the case. For example, the cite for *Rowell v. Holt* is 850 So. 2d 474, meaning the case appears in volume 850 of *Southern Reporter, Second*, beginning on page 474.

An abbreviated version of *Southern Reporter* called *Southern Reporter, Florida Cases* ("Florida Cases") publishes just the Florida cases that appear in the *Southern Reporter*. The pagination in Florida Cases is the same as in *Southern Re-*

Figure 2-3. Excerpt from Case on WestlawNext

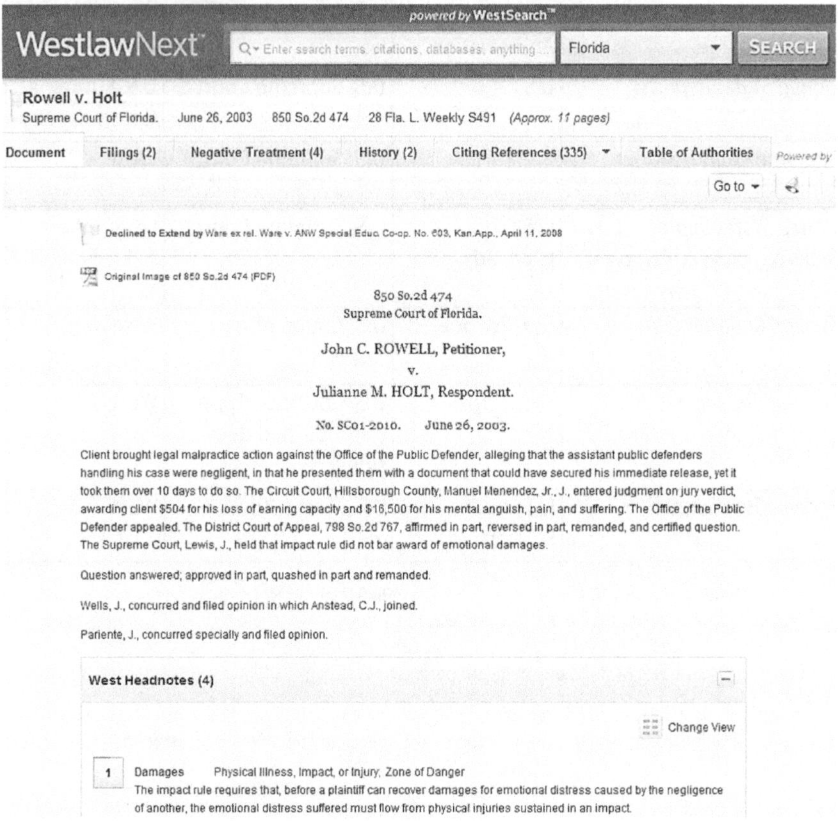

porter, but pages containing cases from Alabama, Louisiana, and Mississippi are omitted.

In addition to the text of the court's opinion, a reporter may include editorial enhancements to aid in research. A case in a West reporter will include a *syllabus* that briefly summarizes the key issues, procedural posture, and holding of the case. The syllabus will be followed by *headnotes*. Each headnote consists of a short paragraph summarizing one discrete point of the case. The syllabus and headnotes are written by the editorial staff of the publishing company, not by the court. These editorial aids should never be cited or relied on as legal authority. Figures 2-3 (online) and 2-4 (print) show an excerpt of a reported case with West editorial enhancements.

Figure 2-4, Part 1. Excerpt from *Southern Reporter*

---

474 Fla.   **850 SOUTHERN REPORTER, 2d SERIES**

twelve years of age, conduct that constitutes the crime of capital sexual battery and carries with it the statutorily mandated term of life in prison.[8] Although the jury was instructed on the lesser included offenses of battery and assault, an instruction on lewd and lascivious assault would have given the jury a basis to convict the defendant of a lesser sex crime.

However, considering the precedent of this Court s opinion in *Hightower*, as well as the trial court s adherence to the Schedule of Lesser Included Offenses set forth in the Florida Standard Jury Instructions in Criminal Cases,[9] I cannot conclude that the trial court erred in denying Welsh an instruction on lewd and lascivious conduct as a permissive lesser included offense of capital sexual battery. Accordingly, I concur with the majority s approval of the First District opinion.

ANSTEAD, C.J., concurs.

---

8. As to Welsh s claim that life imprisonment without the possibility of parole for the crime of capital sexual battery without penile/vaginal union constitutes cruel and unusual punishment, this issue was not addressed by the First District and only summarily briefed in this Court. In my view, the constitutionality of a mandatory punishment of life imprisonment for the specific crime of sexual battery without penile/vaginal union is a significant concern. As the Second District has observed in holding that life imprisonment without parole is not unconstitutional punishment for penile-vaginal capital sexual battery,

[t]here is reason to be concerned that family members who know about the severity of this penalty will hesitate or even refuse to report intrafamily sexual battery, or choose

---

John C. ROWELL, Petitioner,

v.

Julianne M. HOLT, Respondent.

No. SCO1—2010.

Supreme Court of Florida.

June 26, 2003.

Client brought legal malpractice action against the Office of the Public Defender, alleging that the assistant public defenders handling his case were negligent, in that he presented them with a document that could have secured his immediate release, yet it took them over 10 days to do so. The Circuit Court, Hillsborough County, Manuel Menendez, Jr., J., entered judgment on jury verdict, awarding client $504 for his loss of earning capacity and $16,500 for his mental anguish, pain, and suffering. The Office of the Public Defender appealed. The District Court of Appeal, 798 So.2d 767, affirmed in part, reversed in part, remanded, and certified question. The Supreme Court, Lewis, J., held that impact rule did not bar award of emotional damages.

not to cooperate with its prosecution. The eloquent juror in this case demonstrates that jurors who understand the law may choose to exercise their options of jury pardon in some cases. Thus, there is a possibility this inflexible mandatory penalty of life imprisonment may result in fewer convictions for this type of sexual predation than a more flexible penalty. As a result, this more severe punishment may ulitimately prove to be a lesser deterrent than a more flexible penalty.

Gibson v. State, 721 So.2d 363, 370 (Fla. 2d DCA 1998).

9. The Schedule does not list the offense of lewd and lascivious act as a Category 2 (permissible lesser) crime.

Source: *Southern Reporter*. Reprinted with permission of Thomson Reuters. This excerpt contains an example of the caption and syllabus for *Rowell v. Holt*, 850 So. 2d 474 (Fla. 2003).

Figure 2-4, Part 2. Excerpt from *Southern Reporter*

ROWELL v. HOLT   Fla. **475**
Cite as 850 So.2d 474 (Fla. 2003)

Question answered; approved in part, quashed in part and remanded.

Wells, J., concurred and filed opinion in which Anstead, C.J., joined.

Pariente, J., concurred specially and filed opinion.

1. Damages ⊜ 50

The impact rule requires that, before plaintiff can recover damages for emotional distress caused by the negligence of another, the emotional distress suffered must flow from physical injuries sustained in an impact.

2. Damages ⊜ 50.10

The impact rule does not apply to recognized intentional torts that result in predominantly emotional damages, including the intentional infliction of emotional distress, defamation, and invasion of privacy.

3. Damages ⊜ 50

There is no cognizable action for simple negligence resulting in psychological trauma alone, unless the case fits within one of the narrow exceptions to the impact rule.

4. Damages ⊜ 50

Impact rule, which generally requires physical impact before damages can be awarded for negligent infliction of emotional distress, did not bar award of emotional damages to client who was detained for more than 10 days in jail when his public defenders failed to provide court with exculpatory document they had in their possession; special professional duty created by the relationship between client and his attorney, coupled with the clear foreseeability of emotional harm resulting from a protracted period of wrongful pretrial incarceration rendered application of the impact rule unjust and without an underly-

ing justification under the factual circumstances.

———————

Theodore Ted E. Karatinos of Seeley & Karatinos, P.A., St. Petersburg, Florida; and James W. Holliday of Prugh, Holliday & Deem, P.L., Tampa, FL, for Petitioner.

Todd W. Vraspir of Papy, Weissenborn, Poole & Vraspir, P.A., Spring Hill, FL, for Respondent.

Joseph W. Little, Gainesville, Florida; Robert C. Widman, Venice, Florida; and Robert V. Potter, Jr., Clearwater, FL, for Ernest Morgan and Beverly Keehnle, Amici Curiae.

LEWIS, J.

We have for review a decision of a district court of appeal on the following question, which the court certified to be of great public importance:

DOES THE IMPACT RULE APPLY TO PROHIBIT THE RECOVERY OF NONECONOMIC DAMAGES IN A LEGAL MALPRACTICE CLAIM WHEN THE NEGLIGENCE OF A CRIMINAL DEFENSE ATTORNEY RESULTS IN A LOSS OF LIBERTY AND RESULTING EMOTIONAL OR PSYCHOLOGICAL HARM?

Holt v. Rowell, 798 So.2d 767, 773 (Fla. 2d DCA 2001). We have jurisdiction. *See* art. V, ∕ 3(b)(4), Fla. Const. Because we believe the instant case presents a unique factual scenario deserving of an equally tailored principle of law, we rephrase the certified question as follows:

IN AN ACTION FOR LEGAL MALPRACTICE, DOES THE IMPACT RULE PRECLUDE RECOVERY OF NONECONOMIC DAMAGES WHEN THE UNCONTROVERTED NEGLIGENT FAILURE TO DELIVER A

Source: *Southern Reporter.* Reprinted with permission of Thomson Reuters. This excerpt contains the headnotes from *Rowell v. Holt.* The number before each headnote (1–4) is an internal cross reference. The heading before each headnote is the West topic and key number; e.g., "Damages 50" refers to key number 50 within the topic "Damages." Topics and key numbers are explained later in this chapter.

Print reporters evolved as a research tool years before online sources existed, and this has at least two consequences for legal research in the digital age. First, many citation rules continue to require citation to official reporters. Thus, even if you locate your case through one of the online services or a court's website, you may eventually have to check other sources to cite the case correctly. Second, as the courts decided more and more cases, one way of reducing the sheer volume of opinions to be printed was for courts to label some decisions "unreported," "unpublished," or "not for publication." These designations survive, even though many unpublished decisions are now available through online and print sources.[8] Different jurisdictions have different rules governing the precedential effect of unpublished opinions.[9] Some unpublished opinions resemble published opinions in length and complexity. Others are a simple affirmance of a lower court action, without further explanation.[10] An unpublished appellate opinion is typically noted in a table in the appropriate reporter.

B. Digests

A *digest* is a collection of headnotes, arranged by subject, that allows researchers to find cases addressing specific legal topics. West has devised a national digest system that serves as a subject index for all of the West reporters, including regional reporters, federal reporters, and some state reporters. Thus, the West digest system is one of the gateways to reported decisions from all U.S. jurisdictions.

Digests are not limited to West publications and databases. However, the West digest system is the most widely used, and thus familiarity with its features

---

8. Court opinions, even unpublished decisions, have always been available directly from the clerk of the court that decided the case. A written opinion obtained directly from the court clerk is called a *slip opinion* and is referenced by a docket number, which is the number the court assigned the case when it was originally filed.

9. Until 2007, for example, individual circuits in the federal court system decided whether litigants could cite unpublished decisions, and some courts prohibited their use. Since 2007, under Federal Rule of Appellate Procedure 32.1, litigants in the federal courts of appeals have been allowed to cite unpublished opinions of those courts, though each court may determine the weight to give the unpublished opinions. Court rules are covered in Chapter 8.

10. This is typical in Florida, where the district courts of appeal often issue summary affirmances called "PCAs," which means "per curiam affirmance." A PCA is a decision by the court with no written opinion; it has no precedential value and should not be cited, even if you happen to know the case involved an issue similar to the issue you are researching.

is essential. Lexis has created its own set of key terms and headnotes for indexing its case law databases.

1. Organization of the West Digest System

The West digest system is organized around "topics" and "key numbers." Topics form the basis of digest research. There are over 400 topics, covering every area of the law from "Abandoned and Lost Property" to "Zoning and Planning." New topics are added as new areas of law emerge. Key numbers are specific subheadings of each topic. Three key numbers from the topic "Divorce" follow:

> Divorce 91 — Residence of parties
>
> Divorce 93 — Grounds for divorce
>
> Divorce 95 — Prayer for relief

The topics and key numbers used in the West digest system are the same ones assigned to headnotes in West reporters. When you retrieve a case through Westlaw, it contains the same headnotes that would appear in the print version, but they are hyperlinked to the online version of the digest as well. Again, a digest works as an index of case headnotes, arranged by topics and key numbers. Whether you locate relevant topics and key numbers in print or online, they will lead you to all of the cases in your jurisdiction (or others) that have been assigned the same topics and key numbers by West. Because of the ubiquity of West in legal publishing, they will also provide links to secondary sources and legal reference tools.

2. Choosing a Digest

The entire West digest system is accessible through the "Tools" link on West-lawNext. Once you have located a relevant topic within the digest, search options allow you to retrieve state and/or federal cases that have been indexed under that topic, and to limit your research to particular jurisdictions.

When you are working with print sources, you will need to choose the print digest that covers the jurisdiction you are researching. For Florida research, use *West's Florida Digest 2d* (for cases since 1935).[11] *Florida Digest 2d* indexes decisions from Florida state courts and federal courts sitting in Florida.

West publishes digests for other state reporters and some regional reporters. Digests also exist for some specific areas of law. For example, West collects

---

11. The first series of *West's Florida Digest* covers cases through 1935.

cases from various practice areas and publishes them in separate series of reporters. Each practice area reporter would have a digest for that reporter. This collection is useful to a firm practicing in just one area of law, such as social security or bankruptcy; the firm can purchase the smaller collection instead of an entire reporter series and related digest.

For researching an issue involving federal law in print, you will often want to begin with the *Federal Practice Digest*. As its name indicates, this digest includes only federal case law. Because *Florida Digest 2d* includes cases of federal courts sitting in Florida, there is some overlap: those federal cases will also be included in the *Federal Practice Digest*. However, you will not find Florida state cases in the *Federal Practice Digest*. *Federal Practice Digest 4th* and *5th* are the two most recent series of the *Federal Practice Digest*. They index cases starting in 1984 and 2003, respectively.[12]

3. Features of Print Digests

Each West digest contains a "Descriptive-Word Index," which is found at the end of the digest in separate bound volumes. The Descriptive-Word Index is a lengthy topical index that leads to topics and key numbers. When you have located relevant topics and key numbers in the index, use them to search the main digest volumes for potentially relevant cases. Like all volumes in the print digest, each Descriptive-Word Index volume is supplemented with a pamphlet, called a "pocket part," inserted inside the back cover.

West digests also include a Table of Cases, which is helpful when you know a specific party's name, but don't have a case citation. The Table of Cases provides the complete name of each reported case, the citation, a list of relevant topic/key numbers, and the history of the case.

If your research is focused on a specific term or phrase, you can use the "Words and Phrases" volume of the digest to learn whether a court has defined that term or phrase. Words and Phrases leads to a specific subset of the cases found within the main volumes of a digest. The words and phrases are listed alphabetically, followed by references to cases that define them. Each reference includes the full name and citation of the case as well as a short description of the case.

---

12. Earlier editions include *Federal Practice Digest 3d*, which began coverage in 1975; *Federal Practice Digest 2d* (cases from 1961 through November 1975); *West's Modern Federal Practice Digest* (cases from 1939 to 1961); and the *Federal Digest* (cases reported before 1939).

When you know from prior research which topic is likely to contain helpful cases, you may begin your research by going directly to the topic in the main digest volume (topics are arranged alphabetically) and scanning the "Analysis" at the beginning of the topic. This Analysis is a table of contents for all the key numbers within that topic.

III. Finding Cases

Whether you are searching for cases online or using print sources, the basic research method is similar. Start by developing a research vocabulary. Brainstorm your research issue; think of synonyms, antonyms, and related phrases that might lead you to relevant cases. This is always important, but is especially important when you are researching an area of law with which you are not already familiar. Then, as described below, use those terms to search for cases. Use updating tools to verify that the cases you have found are still good law and to find additional authorities.[13]

A. Finding Cases Online

Court opinions are available from many sources, and the resources are constantly improving. Appellate court websites typically post decisions the day they are issued, or within a very short time. In Florida, court websites can be accessed by going to www.flcourts.org. Free or low-cost services are growing in popularity and expanding their coverage. The premium services are Lexis and Westlaw, and they will be the focus of much of the following discussion.[14] However, for reasons of both cost and convenience, it is important to be familiar with some of the alternatives to those providers. Table 1-1 in Chapter 1 lists many online providers of judicial opinions.

---

13. This final step of updating requires the use of citators, which are explained in Chapter 5.

14. Users of this book may encounter Westlaw Classic in the practice setting, although it has been deleted from academic contracts. A primary difference between Westlaw Classic and WestlawNext is the requirement to search Westlaw Classic through particular databases, such as "FL-CS" (Florida Cases). You can search for databases using a box in the left margin, viewing the Westlaw directory, or using the database "wizard." To find a case by citation or party name(s), use the "Find by citation" feature. Some of the limitations that WestlawNext provides through filters can be achieved on Westlaw Classic by using either the "Locate" function or searching "fields" of the document. As an example of field searching, including the name of the author of a treatise in a search query—e.g., au(Padovano)—limits the search to results in which "Padovano" is listed as an author, excluding results where he is merely mentioned.

1. Full-Text Searching

The major advantage of online searching is that it allows researchers to navigate quickly through a huge volume of cases. Most typically this is done through full-text searching—in other words, searching directly in the text of reported cases for research terms.

In its broadest form, full-text searching essentially bypasses indexes or digests. Traditionally, the researcher would select a database corresponding to a particular jurisdiction, and then search within that database for cases that contained specific terms or phrases. This is still how some simpler search engines work. Westlaw and Lexis, however, have developed more sophisticated search mechanisms that allow searching across various databases, so that multiple jurisdictions and multiple types of authority can be retrieved with a single search.

The ability to search the full text of cases is both an advantage and disadvantage of online research. Online searching is extremely efficient if you are looking for a unique term of art or for cases involving an unusual factual situation. If you are searching for general or commonly used terms, however, or are researching an unfamiliar area of law, a full-text search may initially reveal many more cases or authorities than you can reasonably read or analyze for a single issue, including many that are not relevant to the issue at hand. For this reason, becoming proficient in constructing and refining searches is an essential skill for online research.

This section explains how to search online using (a) terms and connectors and (b) natural language. Each has benefits and drawbacks. Terms and connectors searching gives the researcher more control over the search query, but that requires extra effort. Natural language searching is more intuitive, but it cedes control of the search query to the computer.

a. Terms and Connectors Searching

Most legal search engines offer a number of ways to limit or shape search results. These limitations include *connectors*, or symbols that can be used to combine research terms, as well as choices that limit a search result by court, date, and numerous other parameters.

In terms and connectors searching, the researcher selects terms and combines them with connecting or limiting phrases, such as "and," "or," "/10," or "w/10," which means "within 10 words." Other often-used connectors are "/s" or "w/ s," which retrieve cases where specified words appear in the same sentence, and "/p" or "w/p," which retrieve cases where the specified words appear in the same paragraph. Terms can often be grouped using parentheses, allowing the search to incorporate synonyms for key terms. For instance, in a suit against medical professionals, you might include the alternative terms (doctor or physician), telling the computer to find documents containing either of those terms along with others in the search query.

For example, a search for cases where one of the legal issues is the admission of evidence under the "excited utterance" exception to the hearsay rule might look like this:

"excited utterance" /p exception /p hearsay

Searching with terms and connectors allows you to focus your search to find cases most likely to be relevant. If you searched instead for:

"excited utterance" and exception and hearsay

you would retrieve all cases where the three terms appear anywhere—which could include cases analyzing other hearsay exceptions in depth and mentioning excited utterances only in passing.

Connectors are not uniform among different online providers; variations even exist among different services provided by the company. For this reason, it is essential to familiarize yourself with the available connectors when you begin using a new provider.

b. Natural Language Searching

In addition to terms and connectors searching, many legal search engines allow natural language searching—that is, queries written in plain English. These searches rely on complex (and proprietary) algorithms to generate results that appear to be closely matched to your search. The power of the algorithm can affect the results of your search. Some low-cost legal research providers have very simple search engines for natural language searches, but the results could at least get you started with a few relevant cases. On the other end of the scale, WestlawNext and Lexis Advance are so powerful that natural language searches can be very effective.

2. Free Searches and Low-Cost Providers

Because so many decisions are available online, sometimes a simple search in whatever search engine you normally use (e.g., Google, Yahoo!) can be a "quick and dirty" way to jumpstart your case law research. This kind of search will not return a comprehensive result, and you are likely to retrieve many more irrelevant results than relevant results. However, if a quick search leads to even one or two cases on point, those cases can help you expand or refine your research terms for little or no cost. If you are looking for a particular decision and know the parties' names, a quick search using the names as search terms can be an easy way of locating the slip opinion for no cost. This is not, however, a substitute for methodical research using an established provider.

A better, and still free, starting point is Google Scholar (scholar.google.com), which provides access to state appellate and supreme court decisions from 1950 to the present; federal court decisions from 1923 to the present; and United States Supreme Court decisions from 1791 to the present. Searches can be narrowed by jurisdiction on the initial search page and can be further limited by date. The search box also provides the option of using a drop-down menu to focus on key words or phrases. When you click on a specific decision within the search result, the page containing the full text of the document has a link called "How cited"; this link is not a substitute for KeyCiting or Shepardizing, but will indicate how that decision has been treated. You should not build your analysis around a case without updating it using the methods described in Chapter 5.

A number of low-cost online services also provide access to case law. Some of the more popular are Casemaker, Fastcase, Loislaw, and VersusLaw. The competition among these providers, and between the low-cost and premium providers in general, has forced them to develop user-friendly interfaces and some premium features like citators. These services typically provide a variety of search mechanisms, including simple terms and connectors searching. Some of them also support natural language searching. None of the low-cost providers provide access to the range or depth of legal materials available on Westlaw or Lexis. Even their coverage of case law is less extensive than Westlaw's or Lexis's; for example, unpublished opinions are typically not included. Moreover, their citators are computer-generated, rather than generated by legal editors. However, for researching case law and finding the text of statutes, they provide a viable alternative to the premium providers. Their coverage is constantly evolving.

3. Finding Cases on WestlawNext and Lexis Advance

WestlawNext and Lexis Advance provide multiple ways to research cases, some of which have already been introduced. Both services provide a universal search bar that allows you to find a case by its citation, by the party name(s), or through full-text searching. Both also allow you to search databases containing Florida cases, and both provide topic searching. These approaches are described below.

a. WestlawNext

To search for a case by citation or party name(s), simply type that information into WestlawNext's universal search bar. A "Jurisdiction" menu next to the search box allows you to select up to three jurisdictions. This functions as a default until you make a new selection.

A full-text search can be in the form of terms and connectors or natural language. If you select "Florida" from the Jurisdiction menu and run a search in the universal search bar without further limitation, your search result will include Florida cases, statutes, and regulations, along with a variety of commentary sources and practice tools. You can navigate back and forth between the different types of authority in your result using links at the left of the page; an "Overview" link will take you to selected examples of each type of authority in your search result. This type of search can be helpful if you want to browse background information and related content, but is likely to return a large number of results that will not assist in your research without effective use of filters.

You can also use the universal search box to locate specific databases; for example, if you want to search only cases from Florida state courts, you can type "Florida cases" into the universal search bar. WestlawNext will suggest either "Florida State Cases" or "Florida State and Federal Cases." If you select "Florida State Cases," you will then be able to search just in that database. Alternatively, you can use the "Browse" menu underneath the universal search box to navigate to specific sources before running your search.[15]

When the search result appears, a menu bar on the left of the page will give you various options for further narrowing the result. You can "Search within results" using a box that allows you to search for specific terms that occur in your search result. For example, if you have located cases dealing with the excited utterance exception to the hearsay rule and want to limit your result further to cases that arose during the robbery of a store, you could search for the phrase "robbery /s store" within your search result.

As an alternative to full-text searching, the "Tools" link in the Browse menu will take you to the index to the West topic/key number system, so that you can search by topic. The "West Key Number System" is available to browse just as you would in the printed digest. Once you locate relevant topic/key numbers, you can retrieve cases indexed under those numbers. Note that if you have not

---

15. Note that you will arrive at the same place using the following paths: (1) tab for "State Material," then the link for "Florida," and finally the link to "All Florida State Cases"; (2) tab for "All Content," then the links for "Cases" and "Florida," and finally the link to "All Florida State Cases."

selected Florida as your default jurisdiction, then your search in the topic/key numbers will not be limited to Florida cases.

Another way to search cases by topic is to use the "Practice Areas" tab under "All Content." You can select from one of the practice area topics, ranging from "Admiralty & Maritime" to "Tax." Under each practice area, you will find a link to cases dealing with that topic.

b. Lexis Advance

Lexis Advance has similar search features, although there are some differences in detail.

You can use the universal search bar on Lexis Advance to search for cases by citation or by party name(s). Alternatively, enter terms for a full-text search, then limit your search with restrictions available from drop-down menus under the universal search bar. To find Florida judicial decisions, select "Cases" from the menu under "All Content Types," and select "Florida" from the menu under "All Jurisdictions." (You can also navigate to specific sources by selecting "Browse Sources" on the main search screen.)

In the universal search bar, you can enter a natural language search or a terms and connectors search; the "Search Tips" link to the right of the search box lists the available connectors. When your search result is returned it will be broken down by type of authority. A "Snapshot" link will give you examples of selected results in various categories, such as cases, statutes and legislation, and secondary materials; expanded results in all categories will appear under separate tabs. You can narrow your search result using options in the menu bar in the left margin; for example, you can use the options under "Court" to limit your search to decisions issued by the First District Court of Appeal. You can also limit your search to specific "segments" of a decision, such as the judge who authored the opinion, the attorneys who appeared, or the parties. The options for narrowing a search include a "Search within results" box.

One major difference between Westlaw and Lexis is that Lexis does not have a true equivalent of the indexing provided by the West topic/key number system. However, Lexis Advance has its own list of topics that it uses to index case law. From the main search screen you can choose "Browse Topics," which allows you to navigate to specific topics on that list. Most topics have multiple sub-topics. Try to pick the most specific sub-topics that appear to be relevant to your research situation; the Lexis topics are more general than West topics, so retrieving cases indexed under one of the main Lexis topics will often yield unwieldy results.

B. Finding Cases in Print

Finding cases in print sources is a fairly straightforward process. The two major print sources of Florida judicial decisions are the various *Florida Law Weekly* publications, which are typically stored in chronological binders; and *West's Florida Digest*, which leads to cases in *Southern Reporter*. The Florida Rules of Appellate Procedure require cases to be cited to the *Southern Reporter* if the cases are published there, and to the *Florida Law Weekly* if the cases have not yet appeared in the *Southern Reporter*.

1. *Florida Law Weekly*

Florida Law Weekly (FLW) is a source of recent appellate and supreme court cases. This series is published each week online (available only by subscription) and in pamphlets that are kept in binders. FLW is not published by West, so there are no West headnotes and the pagination is not the same as in *Southern Reporter*. However, it is indexed by topic and contains a number of helpful tables that will guide you to cases. If you have a case name, you can consult the Table of Cases; if you are interested in cases applying a particular statute, you can look at the Table of Statutes Construed.

Unlike the *Southern Reporter*, FLW separates the Florida Supreme Court cases from those decided by the district courts. The FLW citation includes an "S" or "D" along with the page number, indicating whether the case appears in the Supreme Court pages or the District Court of Appeal pages.

A related publication, *Florida Law Weekly Supplement*, is the only source for Florida county and circuit court decisions issued after 1991 other than the courts themselves.[16] Proportionately few lower court decisions are published, so often the only source for one of these decisions is the court that decided it. A third publication, *Florida Law Weekly Federal*, reports decisions from the United States Supreme Court, the Eleventh Circuit Court of Appeals, and other federal courts in Florida.

2. *Southern Reporter* and *West's Florida Digest 2d*

To find cases in the *Southern Reporter*, you will typically begin with the Descriptive-Word Index found at the end of *West's Florida Digest 2d*. Skim this index, including the pocket parts for the index volumes, for each of your research terms. Note the topic and key numbers you find there.

---

16. From 1950 to 1991, decisions of some Florida trial courts were reported in *Florida Supplement*. That reporter is no longer published.

Next, use the topics and key numbers to search the main digest volumes. Always refer to more than one topic/key number. Helpful cases may appear at several places in the digest; do not assume that the first successful topic/key number is the only one that will have cases on point. Listed below your topic/key numbers will be headnotes summarizing the portion of each case that is relevant to those topic/key numbers; these are the same headnotes used for the cases in West reporters. Review these case headnotes to determine which cases seem most applicable to your legal problem. Figure 2-5 provides an excerpt from a digest page.[17]

Each headnote begins with the court and date of the decision in bold letters (e.g., **Fla. 2012** for a Florida Supreme Court case decided in 2012). A table near the front of each digest volume contains the abbreviations used in that volume.

After the court abbreviation and date is the text of the headnote. At the end of the headnote is the name of the case and its citation. This information includes the reporter volume, the reporter abbreviation, and the page on which the case begins. When you turn to the case in the *Southern Reporter*, you will find that the exact headnote appears at the beginning of the case, following the topic/key number from the digest.

To find cases that have been decided since a bound digest volume was published, use the Cumulative Annual Pocket Part. Then review any paperback supplement available for your topic/key number.[18] Check the reporter advance sheets, as well; each advance sheet contains its own digest excerpt showing how cases in that advance sheet will eventually be indexed in the digest. Search there for your topic and key number.

In Florida, updating case research beyond the reporter advance sheets requires use of *Florida Law Weekly*. Refer to the issues of FLW that have been published since the most recent reporter advance sheet. The FLW index includes

---

17. Careful readers will notice that a headnote from *Rowell v. Holt*, the case excerpted in Figure 2-4, appears in the right-hand column of Figure 2-5, but that the key number does not match the numbers in Figure 2-4. This is because, on occasion, West renumbers a section of a digest topic to clarify or expand the topic outline. Cases published before the re-numbering still use the former key numbers. However, a table within the digest topic indicates which numbers have changed, so that an older case can still be used as a springboard to find newer, similar cases.

18. The paper supplement will sometimes include cases published even more recently than those included in the pocket part. Sometimes paper supplements are published simply because there is more information than will fit into a pocket part.

Figure 2-5. Excerpt from *Florida Digest 2d*

13A Fla D 2d—153   **DAMAGES** ☞57.18

For references to other topics, see Descriptive-Word Index

anguish caused by arrhythmia that occurred during 26-day period when he was without proper drug, although not for any pain and suffering resulting from his angina, which was not caused by absence of drug. 28 U.S.C.A. §§ 1346, 2671 et seq.

> McLean v. U.S., 613 F.2d 603.

M.D.Fla. 2003. Under Florida law, investors could not recover for emotional distress as part of their compensatory damages in action against investment broker for breach of fiduciary duty, negligent misrepresentation, and fraud, inasmuch as no physical impact was alleged by investors and exceptions to Florida's physical impact rule did not apply.

> Laney v. American Equity Inv. Life Ins. Co., 243 F.Supp.2d 1347.

M.D.Fla. 2002. Under Florida law, allegations that prison bureau's conduct, of allegedly deceiving federal prison inmate's family regarding inmate's terminal medical condition and failing to provide family with reasonable access to inmate during his illness, exacerbated one family member's pre-existing diabetes condition, caused one child to experience difficulty in school, and triggered another child's asthma attacks was insufficient to satisfy impact rule, as required to support a claim for negligent infliction of emotional distress brought by survivors of deceased inmate against United States pursuant to the Federal Tort Claims Act (FTCA). 28 U.S.C.A. §§ 1346, 2671 et seq.

> Gonzalez-Gonzalez-Jimenez de Ruiz v. U.S., 231 F.Supp.2d 1187.

S.D.Fla. 2000. Absent allegation of any physical impact, class of future disabled contest participants could not state claim under Florida law for negligent infliction of emotional distress based upon alleged discriminatory process of selecting individuals to be contestants on network television quiz show through an automated telephone system.

> Rendon v. Valleycrest Productions, Ltd., 119 F.Supp.2d 1344, reversed 294 F.3d 1279, rehearing and rehearing denied 54 Fed.Appx. 493.

S.D.Fla. 1986. Plaintiffs who were passengers on airplane that had to return to airport when engines failed could not recover under Florida law for emotional distress caused by simple negligence, unless plaintiffs could establish discernible physical consequences resulting from their distress, absent allegations of impact or direct physical contact resulting from alleged negligence of airline.

> In re Eastern Airlines, Inc., Engine Failure, Miami Intern. Airport on May 5, 1983, 629 F.Supp. 307, reversed Floyd v. Eastern Airlines, Inc., 872 F.2d 1462, certio-

rari granted 110 S.Ct. 2585, 496 U.S. 904, 110 L.Ed.2d 266, reversed 111 S.Ct. 1489, 499 U.S. 530, 113 L.Ed.2d 569, on remand 937 F.2d 1555.

Fla. 2003. Impact rule, which generally requires physical impact before damages can be awarded for negligent infliction of emotional distress, did not bar award of emotional damages to client who was detained for more than 10 days in jail when his public defenders failed to provide court with exculpatory document they had in their possession; special professional duty created by the relationship between client and his attorney, coupled with the clear foreseeability of emotional harm resulting from a protracted period of wrongful pretrial incarceration, rendered application of the impact rule unjust and without an underlying justification under the factual circumstances.

> Rowell v. Holt, 850 So.2d 474.

Fla. 2002. Impact rule requiring that plaintiff seeking to recover emotional distress damages in negligence action prove that emotional distress flowed from physical injuries plaintiff sustained in impact upon his or her person was inapplicable in cases in which psychotherapist allegedly created fiduciary relationship with patient and breached statutory duty of confidentiality to patient; impact rule should not have been imposed to override clear legislative intent to protect patient from unauthorized disclosure of confidences reposed in psychotherapist, and logical injuries flowing from violation of such protection were emotional in nature. West's F.S.A. § 491.0147.

> Gracey v. Eaker, 837 So.2d 348.

Fla.App. 1 Dist. 2001. Store patron, who sought damages from store owner for humiliation, embarrassment and emotional distress after patron triggered silent alarm and was arrested by police, stated claim for negligence against owner for leaving his store lit and unlocked, creating appearance that store was open, while setting silent burglar alarm.

> Jackson v. Sweat, 783 So.2d 1207, appeal after remand 855 So.2d 1151.

Fla.App. 1 Dist. 1994. Even though shattered glass which fell on tenants' daughter when bomb exploded outside front door of apartment did not injure daughter and black smoke which she breathed were not impact within meaning of physical impact doctrine, daughter was not precluded from bringing negligence action against landlord resulting from explosion; daughter suffered discernable physical injuries which consisted of severe pain, esophageal blockage rendering her unable to swallow, and pain in her joints and elbows, causal relationship between those physical manifestations and psychic injury was supported by competent

† **This Case was not selected for publication in the National Reporter System**
For legislative history of cited statutes, see Florida Statutes Annotated

---

a table identifying whether any decision in that issue of FLW affirms, reverses, or overrules a prior decision. You should also check the topical index to determine whether that issue contains cases on point. Although FLW does not have West's topics and key numbers, by this stage of research you should be able to tell whether a case is potentially on point by skimming the FLW index.

IV. Case Analysis

Throughout the research process, you must analyze the cases you find to decide whether they are relevant to your research problem. If they are relevant, you need to take your analysis a step further to decide what weight to give them.

The type of case analysis lawyers typically study first involves reasoning by analogy. You will find a case concerning the rule of law that applies to your client's situation. Then you will compare the facts of that case to your client's facts. If the essential facts are sufficiently similar, the outcome should be the same. Conversely, if essential facts are dissimilar, the result may be different. Judicial decisions that do not include pertinent facts are not helpful in this process, although they may be cited as support for broad rules of law.

The essential facts are those that the court considered important in reaching its decision. The only way to know this is to read the decision in its entirety. Not every fact noted in the court's summary of the facts (if one exists) is essential. If, for example, the court noted that the plaintiff was a pharmacist, but never mentioned that fact in its analysis, you should not draw conclusions about the relevance of your client's work in a pharmacy based on that case. Other parts of the case may be relevant to your analysis, but pharmacy work is unlikely to be determinative. Similarly, you should not conclude that a fact was essential merely because that fact appears in one of the case headnotes. You must read and analyze the decision itself. Finally, do not assume that cases are factually analogous merely because they are indexed under the same topic and key number.

Analogical reasoning often requires synthesizing, or reconciling, essential facts and principles from several cases. Novice researchers sometimes spend too much time looking for a single case with facts exactly like the facts of their assignment. Often, however, you will have to use multiple cases in analyzing a legal problem, especially if the relevant law contains subparts. For example, in researching negligence, you will learn that this tort has four elements: (1) a duty owed by the defendant to the plaintiff, (2) defendant's breach of the duty, (3) a causal link between the breach and the plaintiff's injury, and (4) injury to the plaintiff. One case may be useful to show whether a duty existed and another case to show whether that duty was breached. Most likely you will have to draw examples from several cases to reach a conclusion about each element. You should not expect to find one perfect case that fully addresses every element of a negligence claim, all within a fact setting very similar to yours.

In addition to the essential facts, the procedural posture of a court decision also plays a role in case analysis. If the issue you are researching is whether your client is likely to prevail on a pretrial motion, such as a motion to dismiss or a motion for summary judgment, you will want to look for cases that were resolved in a similar way, rather than cases in which a full trial was held.

You are also unlikely to find a case or even a group of cases that gives you a definitive answer. Try to focus as much on the reasoning by which you reach your conclusion as on what your conclusion is. Law school professors and supervising attorneys will generally be more concerned with the clarity and completeness of your reasoning than with your ultimate conclusion. It is better to explain your analysis fully, even if you reach a conclusion a professor or supervising attorney may not agree with, than to turn in a memo simply stating what you perceive to be the "right" answer without giving a complete explanation.

Chapter 3

Statutes and Constitutions

State legislatures and Congress pass thousands of statutes each year that address a widening array of subjects, including topics originating in the common law. In addition to applying these statutes to particular disputes, courts may be called upon to determine whether a statute is constitutional. Therefore, many judicial decisions involve statutory interpretation, not merely application of common law principles. You should determine early in your research whether there are state or federal statutes on point and tailor your analysis to address those statutes. Sometimes, although not always, your research will have to include the history of the statute you are interpreting. You should also consider whether your research situation contains issues addressed by the state or federal constitution.

I. An Overview of Statutory Research Terms

In all states, as well as in federal law, a statute begins as a bill that is enacted by the legislature. The bill is typically published not only before it is enacted, but also at different steps along the legislative process. When it becomes law, it is given a new number. Usually the law is published in a chronological compilation of all laws from a particular legislative session. A document containing the text of a new law before it is compiled with other new laws is called a *slip law*, like a "slip opinion" for judicial opinions. The new law may be referred to as a *session law*, a *public law*, or some other similar term. Session laws show how an existing statute was modified by underscoring new language and striking out deleted text.

Volumes of session laws or public laws are not practical to use for most research because they are not organized by subject. Also, in any given year there are many laws in effect in any jurisdiction that would not be covered in the session laws or public laws for that year. As with reporters for judicial opinions, researchers need a way to locate statutes by topic. Thus, each jurisdiction has *codified statutes* that arrange statutes by subject. In Florida, the codified statutes are arranged into chapters, and the chapters are further divided into sections. Unless you are referring to a chapter in its entirety, a Florida statute is referred to as a "section." If you are referring to section 95.04, for example, you would call it "section 95.04," not "chapter 95, section .04."

In some jurisdictions, like Florida, an official codified version of the statutes coexists with unofficial codified statutes from private publishers. The unofficial statutes almost always follow the same codification scheme as the official statutes, but usually also contain annotations of varying lengths. This is true in the federal system as well.

II. Florida Statutory Research

Florida has three codified publications of the state statutes: *Florida Statutes Annotated* (FSA), published by West; *Florida Annotated Statutes*, published by Lexis; and *Florida Statutes*, a state publication.[1] All contain the same statutory language, but *Florida Statutes Annotated* and *Florida Annotated Statutes* include different library aids and case annotations that assist in research. The annotated versions also contain annotated court rules. All three codifications include the text of the state constitution.

Florida Statutes is the official codification of Florida statutory law and must be cited whenever possible. It is available in print and through Online Sunshine, the official website of the Florida State Legislature.[2] Annotated statutes, in Florida and elsewhere, are typically only available through subscriptions or one of the main online providers. The session laws from each year are published in *Laws of Florida*, which is available in print and from the Department of State website.[3]

A. *Florida Statutes*

Although *Florida Statutes* is not annotated, it is often a helpful starting point for research, for three reasons. First, the absence of annotations makes it easier

---

1. The Division of Statutory Revision of the Florida Legislature publishes and indexes the official statutes. *See* § 11.242, Fla. Stat. (2013). The beginning of each volume of *Florida Statutes* contains a preface explaining how the official statutes are revised, adopted, and arranged.

2. Online Sunshine is located at www.leg.state.fl.us/.

3. Online Sunshine includes a link to *Laws of Florida*, or you can go directly to http://laws.flrules.org/.

to skim statutory language in context and move quickly from one section to the next. Second, it is readily available and easy to search on the state legislative website. Third, if you are researching an earlier version of a statute that has been changed (for example, a statute affecting your client's liability for an accident when the statute has changed since the accident occurred), *Florida Statutes* allows you to go directly to the text of the prior version. Online Sunshine has complete versions of *Florida Statutes* dating back to 1997; for older versions, you will need to consult the print volumes.[4] Since 1999, *Florida Statutes* has been republished annually.[5]

To find a statute in *Florida Statutes* when you do not already have a cite, click on "Search Statutes" on the legislative home page and enter a query. The website supports simple Boolean searches. You can also enter a query in the search box that appears at the top of the legislative home page. If you are working in print, begin by looking for research terms in the index, located in the last volume of the set.[6] The research terms listed will give you the section numbers for relevant statutes.

If you know generally that a particular chapter is likely to contain what you are looking for, you can go directly to the table of contents for that chapter, both on the website and in the books. For example, if you are looking for one of the Florida rules of evidence, and you know from your preliminary reading that they are codified in Chapter 90 of *Florida Statutes*, you can go directly to the table of contents for that chapter and skim it.

The end of each section in *Florida Statutes* includes a history note that identifies the number of the session law (or laws) that created and modified that

---

4. At times, because of the updating and reprinting schedule used for the annotated statutes, the text of a previous version of a statute will still be available in one of the print volumes of the annotated statutes. However, you cannot count on the version of a statute from a particular year being easy to discern in the annotated statutes; it makes more sense to go directly to the official statutes for that year.

5. Until 1999, bound volumes comprising the complete statutes of Florida were published in odd-numbered years. In even-numbered years, a two-volume bound supplement was published. The supplement contained the full text of each statute that had been amended or added during the most recent legislative session and tables of statutes changed or repealed. A softbound *Digest of General Laws* updated the bound series each year. From 2003 to 2010 the *Digest of General Laws* was published online. Since then it has been replaced with other online resources, but is still available on the legislative website.

6. If there is a bound supplement for the year you are researching, check the index in volume 2 of that set as well.

Figure 3-1. Sample Statute in *Florida Statutes*

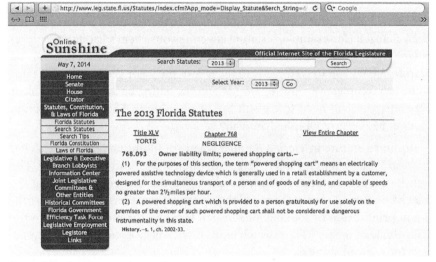

Source: Online Sunshine, www.leg.state.fl.us.

section. An example is shown in Figure 3-1. Explanatory notes are sometimes included as well; for example, statutory sections that have been transferred are followed by a "Note" indicating the former section numbers.[7]

Florida Statutes also has several helpful tables: a Table of Section Changes, a Table Tracing Session Laws to Florida Statutes, and a General Laws Conversion Table linking bill numbers with the corresponding session law numbers. These tables allow you to learn whether the statute you are reading was amended in the most recent legislative session.

For example, assume you have determined section 766.102, a statute relating to medical negligence, relates to your research issue, and you want to know whether it was modified in the most recent legislative session. Look for section 766.102 in the Table of Section Changes. That table tells you that the section was amended by Chapter 2013-108, *Laws of Florida*. Next, the Tracing Table

---

7. Depending on the content and effect of the explanatory note, it may not appear in subsequent versions of the statutes. For example, the Division of Statutory Revision typically eliminates notes regarding effective dates sometime after those dates have passed. The history notes are always included, however, and will alert you to the fact that a change took place in the statutes in a particular year.

tells you that law 2013-108 amended four other sections of *Florida Statutes*; you can skim those sections, as well, because they may be closely related to your issue. Finally, you will use the session law sources described in the next section to see the specific changes in statutory language the legislature made, and learn when they will take effect.

If, on the other hand, you know a bill was passed affecting standards for proving medical negligence, but not where it was codified, you can look up the bill number in the General Laws Conversion Table. From that you will learn the session law number, and when you look in the Tracing Table for that number, you will find where the law was codified.

To find these tables online, click on the "Florida Statutes" link on the legislative website, and then select "Search Statutes" from the menu that appears in the left-hand column.

B. *Laws of Florida* and *West's Florida Session Law Service*

Laws of Florida compiles session laws for each session of the Florida Legislature. A statute's session law number is different from the statute's codified number. An example of a session law number is 2006-15. The first four digits refer to the year of enactment; the other digits are assigned by the Secretary of State to identify the statute and show its location in *Laws of Florida*.[8] In the example above, the statute was enacted in 2006, and it is located in *Laws of Florida* immediately after session law 2006-14. Being assigned consecutive session law numbers does not mean that the subjects of the two statutes are related. The session law number for a statutory provision appears at the end of each provision in both the official and the annotated statutes.

If you are beginning with a session law number and need to find its codified version, use the tables in any one of the codified statutes. Session law 2006-15 is codified in several different places in *Florida Statutes*, including Chapter 216, Planning and Budgeting; Chapter 393, Developmental Disabilities; Chapter 409, Social and Economic Assistance; and Chapter 440, Workers' Compensation. On Westlaw and Lexis, you can search for the session law number in the annotated statutes.

The most direct way to find very recent changes to existing statutes is to use the Tables in the *Florida Statutes* section of the legislative website. In addition,

---

8. For many years a two-digit designation was used. Thus, if you see a reference to a session law numbered 93-415, it was enacted in 1993. The full year has been used since 2000.

while the legislature is in session you should check the "Citator," a daily summary of legislative action, also accessed through the legislative website. Alternatively, you can refer to *West's Florida Session Law Service*. During legislative sessions, this service is produced as a series of soft-cover volumes, allowing for quick publication. You can also update the text of a statute using Westlaw or Lexis.

You will need to work with session laws when you are researching a statute that did not become part of the official code, such as an appropriations bill or budget. Codified statutes do not include session laws that are purely administrative and do not relate to a substantive area of law. In addition, the portion of a session law providing a date on which the law becomes effective is typically not codified, although you can often find that information in the annotated statutes, within the notes following each section. If annotated statutes are not readily available, you may need to consult session laws in connection with the official statutes to determine the effective date of a particular statutory revision.[9] In general, though, you will likely only consult session laws for updating purposes, or when you are tracing changes in the language of a statute.

C. *Florida Statutes Annotated* (West)

When you research Florida statutes on WestlawNext, you are researching in the online version of *Florida Statutes Annotated* (FSA). Westlaw allows you to go directly to the Index and the Table of Contents for FSA, in addition to searching the full text of the statutes.

Full-text searching is especially useful when you have a unique word or phrase in mind. If your search terms do not lead to a manageable result, it may be helpful to search the Index and Table of Contents instead. This will help you focus your research on specific chapters and will also help you refine your search terms.

On WestlawNext, you can access FSA in several ways: typing "Florida Statutes" into the universal search bar; opening "Statutes and Court Rules," then "Florida"; or using the "State" tab to open "Florida," and then "Statutes and Court Rules." The first screen of the database will show the table of contents, and you can expand each title to locate relevant chapters and sections. Alternatively, you can open the statutory index by using a link in the box to the right of the screen. If you already have a citation, you can enter it directly into the universal search bar.

---

9. Even in the official statutes, a very recently codified statute will often have a note clarifying the statute's effective date.

In the print version of FSA, the statutory language is followed by annotations and other editorial notes that aid in research. A sample appears in Figure 3-2.[10]

First are Historical Notes, which show the derivation of the current statute and explain some of its development. The date the statute was enacted and the dates of subsequent amendments are noted, along with the session law numbers. The Historical Notes provide a springboard to legislative history research, discussed later in this chapter. These annotations and notes are also

Figure 3-2. Sample Statute in *Florida Statutes Annotated*

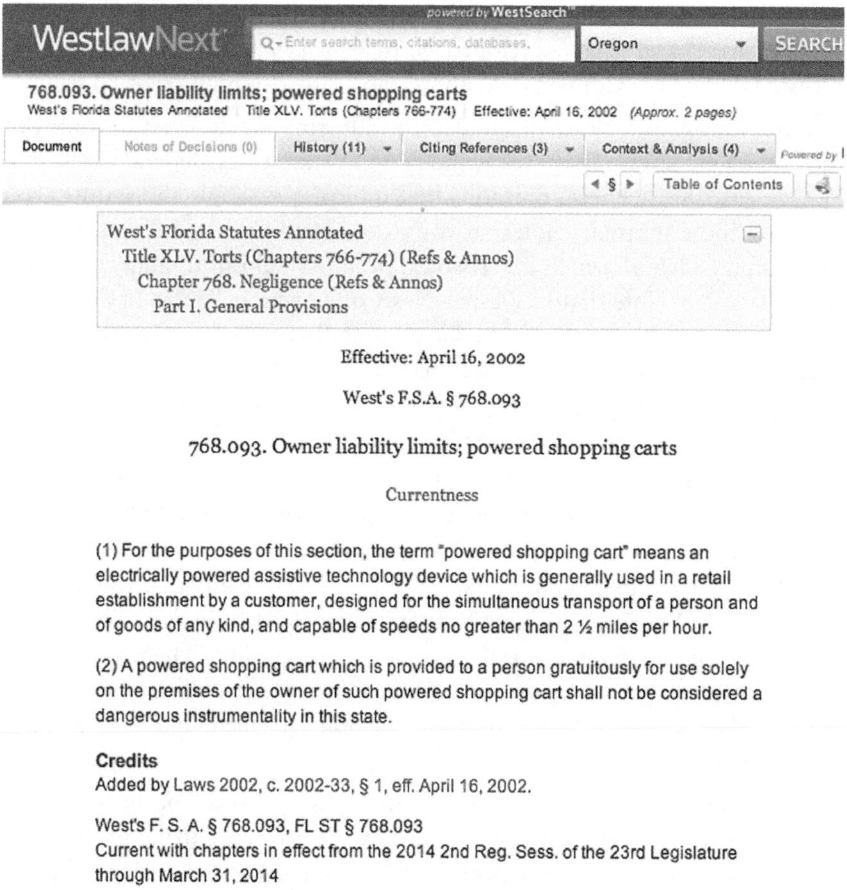

West's Florida Statutes Annotated
Title XLV. Torts (Chapters 766-774) (Refs & Annos)
Chapter 768. Negligence (Refs & Annos)
Part I. General Provisions

Effective: April 16, 2002

West's F.S.A. § 768.093

768.093. Owner liability limits; powered shopping carts

Currentness

(1) For the purposes of this section, the term "powered shopping cart" means an electrically powered assistive technology device which is generally used in a retail establishment by a customer, designed for the simultaneous transport of a person and of goods of any kind, and capable of speeds no greater than 2 ½ miles per hour.

(2) A powered shopping cart which is provided to a person gratuitously for use solely on the premises of the owner of such powered shopping cart shall not be considered a dangerous instrumentality in this state.

Credits
Added by Laws 2002, c. 2002-33, § 1, eff. April 16, 2002.

West's F. S. A. § 768.093, FL ST § 768.093
Current with chapters in effect from the 2014 2nd Reg. Sess. of the 23rd Legislature through March 31, 2014

Source: *Florida Statutes Annotated*. Reprinted with permission of Thomson Reuters.

10. If you are working in an office that has not yet made the transition to WestlawNext, you will see that the Westlaw Classic version of FSA closely resembles the print version in content and organization.

attached to the statutory language in WestlawNext, but are accessed differently. Instead of Historical Notes, WestlawNext lists "Credits" at the end of each section indicating the session laws that created or amended the section. A comprehensive "History" tab for each section gives more extensive background information and provides direct access to the legislative history of the statute you are viewing.

Next in FSA are Cross References to other statutes that relate to or qualify the statute, followed by Law Review and Journal Commentaries, Library References, and Research References. Library References include topic/key numbers that can be used in *West's Florida Digest 2d*; Research References include other West publications that may be relevant to the statute, including *American Law Reports* (ALR) and legal encyclopedias. In WestlawNext, these materials are accessed through a "Context & Analysis" tab at the beginning of each section.

Finally, FSA lists Notes of Decisions: following an alphabetical index of the entries are summary notes, which cite to state cases, federal cases, and Florida Attorney General opinions that interpret or apply the statute. You can skim these summary notes, as you would headnotes in a digest, to get a preliminary idea of which cases would be most helpful in analyzing your statutory issue. Note that in WestlawNext, one or more "notes of decisions" may be selected to appear on the page immediately underneath the statute itself, but the full set of notes is accessed through a "Notes of Decisions" link. Thus, when you are looking at the Good Samaritan Act on WestlawNext, you will see a reference to an Attorney General opinion at the bottom of the page; clicking on the "Notes of Decisions" link will take you to the full set of notes.

When you are reading a statute on WestlawNext, you should immediately update it using the KeyCite link to be sure it has not recently been amended, repealed, declared unconstitutional, or interpreted in a way that would affect your research. WestlawNext has a "Citing References" tab that will take you directly to all citing references for the statute you are reading. The references are exhaustive and, depending on your subscription, some of them may be "out of plan" (that is, not covered by your subscription agreement, and only available for an additional fee).

The print version of FSA is updated with pocket parts. You must refer to the pocket part in the back of the bound volume you are using to see if the statute has been modified or repealed, and to find recent annotations or notes of decisions. Paper supplements called Interim Annotations update the pocket parts. Thus, for complete research in print refer to (1) the bound volume, (2) the pocket part in the bound volume, and (3) any paper supplements.

D. *Florida Annotated Statutes* (LexisNexis)

Florida Annotated Statutes is a relatively new publication designed to compete with *Florida Statutes Annotated*. Its contents are similar to those of FSA, with statutory and constitutional provisions, history notes, and notes of decisions. It provides cross-references to various Lexis practice guides and secondary sources, along with selected cross-references to the Florida Administrative Code.

When you search Florida statutes on Lexis Advance, you are using the online equivalent of *Florida Annotated Statutes*. (Online, Lexis Advance also provides access to a number of municipal codes.) To locate a relevant section, select "Statutes and Legislation" from the drop-down menu under "All Content Types," and then select "Florida" from the drop-down menu under "All Jurisdictions." Then, enter a phrase in the search box. If you have a citation already, you can simply enter that in the search box.

Lexis Advance will return your search result in multiple tabs. One tab will take you to the annotated code. That page will include the text of a statute, followed by history notes, notes of decisions, and links to various secondary sources and practice aids. From there you can browse surrounding sections, or access the table of contents for the entire annotated code. You can also Shepardize the statute from that page. A second tab will take you to a more comprehensive list of sources that cite the statute, with various filter options for targeting specific citing sources, such as jurisdiction.

The print version of *Florida Annotated Statutes* is updated with softcover supplements.

III. Researching the History of State Laws

Legislative history research traces the steps a bill takes from introduction through enactment (or some other resolution). It includes locating documents such as committee reports and floor statements by legislators, as well as committee hearing testimony, all of which may help you understand the general purpose or specific meaning of a statute. It also includes tracking current legislative developments that might affect a client.

Begin your research into the history of an existing state law by familiarizing yourself with the legislative process in that state, using the website of the state's legislature. The legislative process in Florida is outlined below. Although the process is likely to be similar to Florida's, differences in procedure and terminology exist. For example, some states have an "Assembly" instead of a House of Representatives.

State legislature websites typically allow you to check not only the text of current statutes, but also pending bills, along with other information such as committee schedules, amendments to bills, votes, and information on specific legislators. Although the coverage varies from state to state, most legislative websites provide access to the history of recent laws as well. Lexis and Westlaw also have extensive databases for tracking current and recent legislation. State legislative history research for older laws, in general, is more limited.[11] In some instances, answers are not readily available because state documents do not exist or, if they exist, have not been made available online. Some research may require that you locate a legal reference librarian from the state whose law you are researching, or a member of the staff of that state's legislature.

A. The Legislative Process in Florida

The Florida Legislature consists of a Senate and a House of Representatives. The legislature meets in regular sessions beginning each March and lasting two months.[12] After a bill is passed by both houses of the legislature, it is forwarded to the Governor for signature. The bill becomes law—a statute—if the Governor signs the bill or does not veto it within a certain period.

State bills are introduced by a sponsor or multiple sponsors, assigned a bill number, and referred to a committee for discussion and approval or rejection. Legislators can "pre-file" bills before the session begins; the bill will be preliminarily assigned to a committee so that analysis can begin.

Committee work is probably the most important part of legislative history. The most significant documents generated by this process, for legislative history purposes, are the staff analyses that accompany each bill.[13] Staff analyses are

---

11. For example, the Florida Department of State's website currently provides access to *Laws of Florida* dating back to 1997.

12. The legislature can vote to extend the sessions or, in special circumstances provided for by law, call a special session. Special sessions are more typically "proclaimed" by the Governor and are not extensions of the regular session, but are convened to address a specific issue.

13. *See, e.g.*, Carol A. Roehrenbeck, *Florida Legislative Histories: A Practical Guide to Their Preparation and Use* 15–17 (1986) (discussing the uses of legislative history by Florida courts). The Florida Senate currently prints a disclaimer on each staff analysis that purports to limit the use of the staff analysis as evidence of a bill's legislative history; in practice, however, the staff analyses continue to be consulted regularly.

sometimes referred to as "committee reports"; they are prepared by the committee to which a bill is assigned and may include such information as goals of the legislation, potential effects of the legislation, and a summary of the state of the law without the legislation. They may also include "fiscal notes" or "economic impact statements." A copy of a staff analysis is included in the appendix to this chapter.

The committee to which a bill is assigned may also hold hearings in which citizens, organizations, or experts are invited to speak about the bill. These hearings are recorded, but not routinely transcribed.

If the committee approves the bill, it goes to the main floor of the House or Senate, where it is debated, possibly amended, and voted on. These debates and amendments are additional tools for interpreting the legislative history of a statute.

The Senate and House must both pass a bill before the bill is forwarded to the Governor for signature, but a bill may originate in either house. When the Senate and House pass different versions of a bill, the bill may be assigned to a conference committee to work out the differences. Sometimes a bill that originated in one chamber will be substituted for a similar bill in the other. Votes, floor amendments, committee action, and substitutions are all recorded in the daily *Journal of the Senate* and *Journal of the House of Representatives*.

If the Governor signs a bill or does not veto a bill within a specified time period, it becomes law. When the Governor vetoes a bill, he sends a statement of his objections to the bill back to the house where the bill originated. The statement will also appear in the *Journal* of that house.

Online Sunshine contains numerous resources for tracing the path a particular bill took to become a law. On the legislative home page is a link to the "Citator," from which you can trace the history of bills that became law, dating back to 1998. The Senate and House websites, in addition, have links to legislative history documents such as Staff Analyses. For Senate bills, start with the "Session" tab on the Florida Senate home page, which will take you to links to legislative history documents for the last several sessions. Older materials, including *Journals* dating back to 1839, are available through the Senate Archives at archive.flsenate.gov. For House bills, go to the "Documents" tab on the Florida House of Representatives website.

B. Researching Pending Legislation: Bill Tracking

Often you will need to follow the progress of a pending bill from its introduction, through committee action or approval, to any ultimate disposition.

This is called "bill tracking" and uses many of the same tools used to research the history of existing laws. Florida bill tracking information is available through both print and online sources. Online Sunshine is probably your best and fastest source for checking legislative information. Simply go to www.leg.state.fl.us and follow the links for the Senate or House to access committee information, bill summaries, bill text, statistical reports, and other research tools. Lexis and West-law also have bill tracking databases, which can be helpful if you are going to be searching other databases as well; for current legislative developments, how-ever, the legislative website is a better starting point.

Another source of legislative information is the "Citator" on the home page of the legislative website. This is updated daily when the legislature is in session and is a useful device for bill tracking. It includes a History of Senate Bills and History of House Bills, arranged by bill number. Following each bill number is a summary of all action on a particular bill. Unlike the *Journals*, the history links will not tell you which legislators supported the bill, but give only the results of votes. The Citator also has a table of *Florida Statutes* references for bills and an index of bills by subject. At the end of each legislative session (whether regular or special), the legislature publishes a cumulative volume for that session. This volume was formerly called *History of Legislation* and is now titled *Final Legislative Bill Information*. It is available through Online Sunshine for each legislative session from 1998 to the present.

The best source of substantive information on a pending bill is often the committee to which the bill was assigned or the office of the bill's sponsor. Do not overlook newspaper or magazine articles, which can be good sources of background information on a particular bill.

C. Researching the History of Existing Laws

To research the history of a statute that has already been enacted and codified, you will have to find the bill number for that statute by looking in *Laws of Florida* under the appropriate session law number. Remember that session law numbers are assigned to Florida bills in the order in which they are passed by the legislature and that you find them in the notes at the end of each statutory section in *Florida Statutes*, *Florida Statutes Annotated*, or *Florida Annotated Statutes*.

Once you have the bill number, trace the bill's progress by consulting *Final Legislative Bill Information* or *History of Legislation*, and noting information such as the name of the committee that handled the bill and the dates on which any action occurred. You might also check the *Journals* for the text of any floor amendments to your bill. For relatively recent bills, you can accomplish much of this work through the Florida legislature website.

The commercial research providers also provide links to some Florida legislative history documents. If you are viewing a statute on WestlawNext, clicking on the "History" tab while you are viewing the statute will take you to legislative history links. If you are viewing a statute on Lexis Advance, the Shepard's result for that statute will take you to the session laws that created or modified the statute; Lexis Advance also has a "Florida Legislative Bill History" database, but its coverage is more limited than Westlaw's databases for legislative history. Note, however, that with either provider, some documents may not be covered by your subscription; in that case, or for any bills passed before 1998, you will have to use print sources.[14]

Legislative committee records are typically held by the committee for a year (although some committees hold records for longer than that) before being forwarded to the Capitol Branch of the State Library (formerly the Legislative Library, located at the Florida Capitol) for processing. From there, the records are sent to the Florida State Archives, located in the R.A. Gray Building in Tallahassee, which maintains files of legislative documents dating back to 1969.[15] Documents are accessed at the State Archives by bill number or session law number.

In addition to these legislative materials, consider researching case decisions or secondary sources, including legal newspapers, discussing your statute. Sometimes a law review or bar journal article will contain information on concerns the legislature addressed when passing a particular bill. Journals or newsletters of advocacy organizations can also provide background information on legislation of interest to those organizations. While none of these sources are legislative history documents, they can provide helpful context and background information.

The *Florida Style Manual*, published by the *Florida State University Law Review* and available online, contains specific citation forms for staff analyses, committee reports, and other legislative materials.

---

14. Until the late 1990s a private publisher, Florida Information Associates, Inc., published selected legislative materials. These included a set of staff analyses for bills that had become law, stored on microfiche. A local law library or university library may have access to this set of materials; search for "Florida Information Associates" to see what your library's holdings are.

15. Visit the website of the State Archives for more information on the procedures to follow when searching for archival materials: http://dlis.dos.state.fl.us/archives/legislativeresearch.cfm.

IV. Federal Statutory Research

Federal statutory research is similar to state statutory research, but is often facilitated by the extensive federal materials available online. Table 3-1 lists a few of many websites giving researchers quick access to federal statutes, bill tracking, and legislative history as well as to regulations, agency information and reports, and other information.

Table 3-1. Essential Websites for Federal Legislative Research

---

Library of Congress—Congress.gov
- Full text of bills and resolutions
- Summary information about bills and resolutions
- *Congressional Record*: 1995–present
- Committee reports: 1995–present
- Presidential nominations
- Treaties

**Federal Digital System of
Government Publishing Office (GPO)**—www.gpo.gov/fdsys/
- *United States Code*
- *Code of Federal Regulations*
- *Federal Register*
- *Congressional Record*
- Compilation of Presidential Documents

United States House of Representatives—www.house.gov
- Current legislative information

United States Senate—www.senate.gov
- Current legislative information

U.S. Department of Commerce—http://fedworld.ntis.gov/govlinks.html
- Government and agency websites
- Federal employment information

A. Federal Statutes

The official codification of federal laws is the *United States Code* (USC), which must be cited whenever possible. The print version of the USC is formally republished in its entirety every six years and updated with supplemental paper volumes between publication dates. Online versions of the USC are frequently updated; the main reasons to pay attention to official publication dates are, first, to be sure the provision was in effect at the time period you are researching, and second, for purposes of legal citation. For finding and updating statutory language, you can use one of the many online versions of the USC.

Almost all federal statutory research is conducted using one of the two major annotated codes: *United States Code Annotated* (USCA) and *United States Code Service* (USCS). The annotated federal codes contain the language of the statutes, historical information, and extensive, but not identical, annotations.

West publishes USCA, so that series cross-references a variety of West publications. It also includes cross references to USCCAN, a legislative history research tool discussed below. When you search for federal statutes on WestlawNext, you are using the online version of USCA. LexisNexis publishes USCS, so that version is available online through Lexis Advance. While USCS contains similar information, the annotations are not identical to those found in West products and include references to secondary sources not included in USCA, as well as some agency rules and decisions.

Some practitioners prefer one series to another and, for a truly comprehensive look at both the history and interpretation of a federal law, you may need to consult both. For purposes of finding statutory text and cross references to other sources, however, either is helpful. In print, both USCA and USCS are updated using pocket parts and supplementary pamphlets. Each annotated code contains a "Popular Name Table" in addition to a topical index.

When taking notes on federal statutory research, remember that you will need to record both a title number and a section number for each relevant statute. For example, the federal statute on diversity jurisdiction is found in Title 28, Section 1332. Because federal statutes are codified in over 50 titles, each subdivided into sections, it is critical that you note both numbers in your research.

B. Federal Session Laws

In the federal system, new laws are given "public law numbers" instead of "session law numbers." While the Florida session law number tells you the year a statute was passed, a public law number tells you the number of the Congress that passed the bill: Pub. L. 108-405, for example, is the 405th bill passed by the 108th Congress. You cannot tell from the public law number alone that it was passed in 2004. Like Florida session laws, federal public laws contain the text of a statute as it was enacted, but not necessarily as it will be codified in the *United States Code*. New federal laws are officially compiled in *United States Statutes at Large*. The easiest way to find recent public laws is through using one of the federal legislative websites in Table 3-1.

V. Researching the History of Federal Laws

Before starting to compile a legislative history of a federal bill, do some preliminary research to see if the work has already been done. Although more often than not you will have to do the research yourself, you will sometimes find legislative history already compiled for major legislation (for example, the Occupational Safety and Health Act).[16] Law review articles or other legal periodicals may be helpful starting points for researching a federal bill if the topic was of interest to scholars or practitioners.

Federal legislative history sources are widely available online. The official site for federal legislative information is Congress.gov, described below, which has extensive information on current legislation and recent legislative history. Both Westlaw and Lexis have federal legislative history databases, as well. These databases can be searched directly, or you can access documents relating to a specific statutory provision using the "History" link or tab while you are viewing that provision. Coverage is not uniform and changes frequently.

A. Congress.gov

Congress.gov provides thorough information on pending legislation, including information on sponsors and cosponsors, amendments, committee assignments, and votes, as well as links to related bills. It also provides access to the *Congressional Record*, a daily record of the proceedings of the House and Senate, from 1995 to the present. Committee reports are also available from 1995 to the present. You will need other sources to perform thorough

---

16. One recognized source for these compilations is Nancy P. Johnson, *Sources of Compiled Legislative Histories* (2d ed. 2012). Search your library's holdings for "compiled legislative histories" to find other sources.

research into the history of a particular law, but this website is a good starting point unless your research involves an older law.

B. ProQuest Congressional

ProQuest Congressional is a fee-based collection, available through many law libraries, that provides full-text searching of federal legislative history documents. It incorporates the material formerly published by the Congressional Information Service (CIS). For many years CIS was the unofficial, but most comprehensive, source of legislative history documents for federal bills. CIS indexed and abstracted bills, committee reports, hearings, and other documents, and made the full text of each of these documents available on microfiche, starting in 1970. An even older series, the *United States Congressional Serial Set*, has been publishing House and Senate Documents and House and Senate Reports since 1817. Portions of the *Serial Set* have been digitized for public access and can be viewed through the Library of Congress website at http://memory.loc.gov/ammem/amlaw/lwss.html. However, the majority of the series is not yet searchable without a subscription.

C. *United States Code Congressional and Administrative News* (USCCAN)

USCCAN reports the results of each session of Congress, including laws, presidential proclamations, executive orders, and other actions. The series is available for full-text searching on WestlawNext. In print, the volumes corresponding to each session are divided into two parts subtitled *Laws* and *Legislative History*. USCCAN *Laws* reprints the full text of each statute as it would appear in *United States Statutes at Large*, which is the official session law service for Congress, and includes cross references to *Statutes at Large* citations. USCCAN *Legislative History* reprints selected documents from the law's history, such as committee reports. It also includes separate legislative history tables for each law. USCCAN is arranged by public law number and provides easy references to bill numbers for each public law.

USCCAN is a useful starting point for legislative history research because it is accessible and easy to use, and because the legislative history tables provide a convenient checklist for gathering documents. However, USCCAN is a selective collection of legislative history documents; thorough research still requires reference to other sources.

D. *Congressional Record*

The *Congressional Record* (CR) is a chronological publication containing transcripts of legislative debate; the text of bills and any amendments; and voting records. It is indexed by subject, legislators, and titles. Despite the objective-sounding name, entries in the CR are subject to revision and amendment from legislators. Other sources, such as committee reports, are generally given more weight in legislative histories. The CR is still a helpful source for developing a general understanding of how a particular law was enacted. When Congress is in session, the CR is published daily. At the end of each Congress, the daily editions are compiled in a "permanent" edition for that Congress with different pagination.

The most straightforward way to search the CR is through Congress.gov, which provides access to the CR dating back to 1995. For previous years, Westlaw and Lexis provide coverage dating back to 1985; before that, you will need to use one of the print indexes to the CR.

VI. Statutory Interpretation

Statutory interpretation begins with a careful reading of the statute. Never rely on an article's summary of a statute or even a court's quote of a statute as a replacement for reading the statute yourself.

Do not focus too narrowly on a single section or subsection before you understand the context in which it applies. For example, if you are researching a particular sub-section of Florida Statutes, look at the contents of the chapter in which it is codified. Then, read the entire section. Note whether the section specifies any definitions or effective dates. Sometimes a statute will incorporate definitions from another section; in that case, you will need to read the definitions section as well.

Next, read through the statute slowly, noting important requirements or exceptions, and marking out provisions that clearly do not apply to your client's circumstances. Pay special attention to tiny words that can change the meaning of the statute. Note the difference between "and" — "or"; "all" — "some"; "must" — "may." Read the statute again, focusing this time on the relevant portions. If the statute is complex, outlining the rule presented in the statute may increase your understanding of it. Table 3-2 demonstrates one way of outlining a statute.

Review the statute frequently as you continue your research. This review will ensure that you remember the exact language of the statute and will allow you to bring to subsequent readings greater insight based on your increased knowledge.

A. Interaction Between Statutes and Cases

After identifying the relevant portions of the statute, the next step is to find cases relevant to that statute and use them to refine your understanding of the statute and its application to your facts.

Consider the example in Table 3-2, a statute creating immunity from liability for people who act as "good Samaritans" at the scene of certain emergencies. The statute was passed to address a matter of public concern, namely the fear that rendering assistance to an injured or ill person during an emergency may expose the rescuer to liability later if the injured or ill person does not fully recover. The risks and costs of this exposure are weighed against the risk that a person who is injured by an unskilled or careless rescuer will have no way to recover damages. The legislature eventually drafted a statute that created immunity if certain specified conditions are satisfied.

Table 3-2. Outlining a Statute

Example

Sec. 768.13, Fla. Stat. (2013) Good Samaritan Act; immunity from civil liability.—

    (2)(a) Any person, including those licensed to practice medicine, who gratuitously and in good faith renders emergency care or treatment either in direct response to emergency situations related to and arising out of a public health emergency declared pursuant to s. 381.00315, a state of emergency which has been declared pursuant to s. 252.36 or at the scene of an emergency outside of a hospital, doctor's office, or other place having proper medical equipment, without objection of the injured victim or victims thereof, shall not be held liable for any civil damages as a result of such care or treatment or as a result of any act or failure to act in providing or arranging further medical treatment where the person acts as an ordinary reasonably prudent person would have acted under the same or similar circumstances.

Outline

What must be true for a person to be immune from liability under this statute?

- the person's act (or failure to act) must be gratuitous
- the person must act in good faith
- the emergency care must be either one of the following
    - in response to a legally declared public health emergency, or
    - in response to a legally declared state of emergency, or
    - at the scene of some other emergency that is outside of a hospital, doctor's office, or other place with proper medical equipment
- the victim must not object
- the person must act as an "ordinary reasonably prudent person" would, given the circumstances

Like many statutes, this statute includes language that can cover a broad array of situations that may arise in the future: it protects a rescuer from liability if that person "acts as an ordinary reasonably prudent person would have acted under the same or similar circumstances." What an ordinary, reasonably prudent person would do is left open for a case-by-case determination. Eventually, when a dispute emerges over the application of that general statute to a specific situation, a court will have to interpret the statute and decide whether, in a specific factual situation, the rescuer acted as an ordinary reasonably prudent person would have acted.

Sometimes a statute codifies an existing common law principle. In this situation, previous cases will exist that did not consider the statute, even though they address an issue similar to the statutory issue you are researching. Whether these prior cases are relevant in interpreting the new statute will depend in large part on whether the cases and statute are closely aligned, or whether the statute was enacted to change some aspect of the common law principle.

Other times, a statute may be enacted to overrule something a court has done. In such a situation, the older cases will not be binding, but they may provide insight into the legislature's intent.

B. Statutory Construction and the Use of Legislative History

Courts have developed rules, sometimes called "canons of construction," for interpreting statutes. One of the most basic canons is that statutes should be interpreted according to their "plain meaning." Courts should read the words of the statute, give them their ordinary meaning, and apply them to the facts of the case. Only when the words of a statute are ambiguous or would lead to absurd results if followed literally should courts refer to sources beyond the four corners of the statute, such as legislative history documents.

When seeking to use legislative history to advocate for a particular interpretation of a statute, you should be aware of how and when courts in your jurisdiction will be receptive to an argument based on "legislative intent." Your brief must be tailored to your audience and your issue. Some courts are more receptive than others to arguments based on legislative history. Some issues of statutory interpretation do not require the use of legislative history.

The Florida Supreme Court has often said that ambiguity is a prerequisite to any inquiry into the "intent" of the statute.[17] Only where a court finds a

---

17. *E.g., State v. Egan*, 287 So. 2d 1, 4 (Fla. 1973). Florida courts often cite *State v. Egan* for the proposition that ambiguity is required before a court can go beyond

statute is ambiguous can it inquire into the statute's legislative history.[18] However, the Florida Supreme Court has also stated that courts may consider evidence of legislative intent where there are "cogent reasons" suggesting that the terms, alone, do not accurately reflect that intent, and where ignoring the legislative intent would lead to unreasonable results.[19] When writing a brief to a Florida court, you need to frame your argument in terms of these standards and use the appropriate vocabulary. Another jurisdiction may have a slightly different vocabulary; it is your responsibility as an advocate to do the necessary research into the standards applied in each jurisdiction to enable you effectively to present your client's case. Moreover, a court's approach to statutory construction can evolve over time.[20]

Finally, you should remember that various legislative sources are not given the same weight when construing statutes.[21] Although materials such as hearing transcripts and records of debate may add to your understanding of the background of the statute you are researching, they are not usually considered authoritative for interpreting the bill as passed by the legislature.[22] Many of the

----

the plain meaning of a statute in ascertaining its meaning. *E.g., Westphal v. City of St. Petersburg*, 122 So. 3d 440, 457 (Fla. 1st DCA 2013).

18. *Williams v. State*, 121 So. 3d 524, 530 (Fla. 2013) ("When a statute is clear, this Court need not look behind the statute's plain language for legislative intent or resort to rules of statutory construction to ascertain intent."); *Weber v. Dobbins*, 616 So. 2d 956, 958 (Fla. 1993) ("The cardinal rule of statutory construction is that the courts will give a statute its plain and ordinary meaning.") (citation omitted).

19. *Weber*, 616 So. 2d at 958.

20. *See generally* Stephen Breyer, *On the Uses of Legislative History in Interpreting Statutes*, 65 S. Cal. L. Rev. 845 (1992) (arguing against an "abandonment" of legislative history as an aid to construction). Justice Breyer identifies the following "correct" uses of legislative history, listed from the least to most controversial: clarifying ambiguity, avoiding absurd results, correcting drafting errors, taking account of specialized meanings given to certain terms, identifying the "reasonable purpose" underlying a particular term or provision, and choosing between different interpretations of a controversial statute. *Id.* The article contains illustrations of each category drawn from his experience on the bench.

21. Carol A. Roehrenbeck, *Florida Legislative Histories: A Practical Guide to Their Preparation and Use* 16–17, n.5 (1986), noted that of the 46 Florida appellate decisions citing legislative materials between 1971 and 1985, 41% cited committee reports and staff analyses; other cited materials, in decreasing order by frequency of citation, were bills or resolutions, House and Senate *Journals*, hearings, debates, and Governor's statements.

22. The First District Court of Appeal emphasized the unreliability of statements made during floor debate as a source of legislative intent in *Smith v. Crawford*, 645 So. 2d 513, 525 n.8 (Fla. 1st DCA 1994).

documents you find in the course of your research will not be highly persuasive; legislative history research, like all legal research, is a process, and these documents have value as steps in that process.

C. Other Canons of Construction

There are a number of other canons of construction in addition to the "plain meaning" example discussed above. You should not be surprised to see canons that appear to be contradictory. In fact, almost every rule of construction can be countered with another. For example, one court might interpret a statute according to the rule that "expressing one thing excludes another." Under this rule, the court might construe a statute that lists "cats, dogs, and birds" to exclude ferrets. Another court might interpret the same statute according to the rule that examples mentioned in a statute for purposes of illustration do not limit the statute's application; the second court might reason that "cats, dogs, and birds" were illustrations of household pets and decide that the statute included a ferret that was kept as a household pet.[23]

Although there are general similarities in these rules from one jurisdiction to the next, you should be familiar with the canons as they are most often applied in your jurisdiction.

VII. Constitutional Research

Like the constitutions of many states, the Florida Constitution is much more specific than the United States Constitution. While the Florida Constitution contains broad guarantees analogous to those in the U.S. Constitution, including the right of religious freedom[24] and protection from unreasonable searches and seizures,[25] the Florida Constitution specifically provides a right to privacy[26] that is only implied in the U.S. Constitution. Moreover, the Florida Constitution addresses some issues that you might expect to find instead in statutes, such as a 2002 provision limiting the size of classes in public schools.[27]

---

23. For a chart comparing 28 pairs of canons of construction, see Karl N. Llewellyn, *Remarks on the Theory of Appellate Decision and the Rules or Canons About How Statutes are to be Construed*, 3 Vand. L. Rev. 395 (1950).

24. Art. I, § 3, Fla. Const.

25. *Id.* § 12.

26. *Id.* § 23.

27. *Id.* Art. IX, § 1.

Because so many areas of law are covered by the Florida Constitution, you are likely to need to research constitutional provisions at some point. Constitutional research is very similar to statutory research. You must find the relevant constitutional provision, read the provision carefully, and find cases and other authorities that interpret or apply the provision.

For finding the text of a provision, you can go to the full text of the Florida Constitution on Online Sunshine, or in the final volume of the print version of *Florida Statutes*. For most constitutional research, one of the annotated statutory codes will be a better place to begin. Volumes in each series, and in their online counterparts, contain the text of the constitution and, for each provision, the annotations noted above in the discussion of statutory research. Remember to update your research using the methods you would use to update statutory research. The Florida Constitution is also available on Westlaw and Lexis.

Article XI provides for the revision of the Florida Constitution every twenty years. In 1997–98, the Constitution Revision Commission, created pursuant to Article XI, section 2, proposed a number of amendments to the Florida Constitution. An overview of this commission and a summary of its work are available at www.law.fsu.edu/crc. Proposed changes to the state constitution are typically covered in both legal and non-legal newspapers, as well as in other commentary sources; therefore, secondary source research is likely to be helpful as well.

Both USCA and USCS include the U.S. Constitution in the first few volumes of the series, and WestlawNext and Lexis Advance both provide access to the U.S. Constitution. Each offers an index specific to the Constitution, and the online versions obviously provide full-text searching. A vast body of case law and commentary has developed to interpret various federal constitutional provisions. In addition, the U.S. Constitution is the subject of numerous treatises and commentaries. After you identify a relevant article, section, or amendment and read the text, your research will probably progress more quickly and be more focused if you refer to secondary sources early in your research.

Appendix: Staff Analysis

The following is an excerpt from an analysis of a bill that was passed in 2013, the "Freedom from Unwarranted Surveillance Act." This staff analysis would be cited as Fla. S. Comm. on Crim. Just., SB 92 (2013) Staff Analysis (rev. Jan. 10, 2013). The full excerpt can be viewed at http://www.flsenate.gov/Session/Bill/2013/0092/Analyses/2013s0092.pre.cj.PDF.

The Florida Senate
BILL ANALYSIS AND FISCAL IMPACT STATEMENT
(This document is based on the provisions contained in the legislation as of the latest date listed below.)

Prepared By: The Professional Staff of the Committee on Criminal Justice

BILL: SB 92

INTRODUCER: Senator Negron

SUBJECT: Searches and Seizures

DATE: January 10, 2013   REVISED:

	ANALYST	STAFF DIRECTOR	REFERENCE	ACTION
1.	Cellon	Cannon	CJ	**Pre-meeting**
2.			JU	
3.			ACJ	
4.			AP	
5.				
6.				

I.   Summary:

Senate Bill 92 creates the "Freedom from Unwarranted Surveillance Act."

The bill prohibits law enforcement agencies, as defined by the bill, from using drones to gather evidence or other information with one exception for certain risks of terrorist attack. The term "drone" is defined by the bill.

Any evidence gathered in violation of the bill is inadmissible in a criminal prosecution in any court of law in this state. Provisions are made in the bill for civil actions by an aggrieved party against a law enforcement agency that violates the prohibitions in the bill.

The bill becomes effective July 1, 2013.

This bill creates a new section of the Florida Statutes.

II.   Present Situation:

Drones Historically Utilized by Military in Warfare, Hostile Situations

Drones, also called Unmanned Aerial Vehicles and Unmanned Aerial Systems, will be referred to as "drone" in this bill analysis.

Although drones were utilized as far back as the war in Vietnam, the term "drone" has recently become part of the vernacular since the use of drones by the U.S. military has become more common knowledge among the civilian population.[1] Because drones are unmanned aircraft, they are especially useful in search and destroy missions where military personnel would otherwise be placed in harm's way.

Drones are also highly capable of gathering military intelligence because drones can be quite stealthy and they can carry sophisticated surveillance equipment. For example, the U.S. Army recently acquired a 1.8 gigapixel camera to use on its drones which can track objects on the ground from 65 miles away while the drone is flying at an altitude of 20,000 feet.[2]

Drones can be equipped with infrared cameras,[3] license plate readers[4] and "ladar" (laser radar).[5] It has been reported that in 2011 the U.S. Army contracted with two corporations to develop facial recognition and behavioral recognition technologies for drone use.[6]

Drones range in size from wingspans of six inches to 246 feet and can weigh from approximately four ounces to over 25,600 pounds.[7] They may be controlled manually or through an autopilot which uses a data link to connect the drone's pilot to the drone.[8]

Non-Military Drone Flight in the United States

There is usefulness for drones not just militarily but domestically as well. As far back as 2007, the Federal Aviation Administration (FAA) was aware of approximately 50 companies, universities, and government organizations developing and producing some 155 drone designs in the United States alone.[9]

Drones have been used in a multitude of tasks by U.S. government agencies, and in other countries. The first non-military use of drones by a government agency came in 2004 when the U.S. Customs and Border Patrol began to utilize them.[10] In February 2010, the U.S. Customs and

---

[1] *Unmanned Aerial Vehicles Support Border Security*, Customs and Border Protection Today, July 2004, www.cbp.gov/xp/CustomsToday/2004/Aug/other/aerial_vehicles.xml.

[2] *Drones in Domestic Surveillance Operations*, Congressional Research Service, September 6, 2012, www.fas.org/sgp/crs/natsec/R42701.pdf.

[3] These cameras are capable of "seeing" based upon the relative levels of heat in its viewing area. For example, see http://www.draganfly.com/uav-helicopter/draganflyer-x6/features/flir-camera.php.

[4] *Drones in Domestic Surveillance Operations*, Congressional Research Service, September 6, 2012, www.fas.org/sgp/crs/natsec/R42701.pdf; *Unmanned Aerial Vehicles Support Border Security*, Customs and Border Protection Today, July 2004, www.cbp.gov/xp/CustomsToday/2004/Aug/other/aerial_vehicles.xml.

[5] "Ladar" is reported to produce three-dimensional images and has the capability to "see" through trees and foliage. *Drones in Domestic Surveillance Operations*, Congressional Research Service, September 6, 2012, www.fas.org/sgp/crs/natsec/R42701.pdf; U.S. Army, UAS Center for Excellence, *Eyes of the Army, US Army Roadmap for Unmanned Aircraft Systems 2010-2035* (2010).

[6] Clay Dillow, Popular Science, September 28, 2011, popsci.com/technology/article/2011-09/army-wants-drones-can-recognize-your-face-and-read-your-mind.

[7] 14 CFR Part 91, Docket No. FAA-2006-25714, Department of Transportation, Federal Aviation Administration, Unmanned Aircraft Operations in the National Airspace System, February 6, 2007.

[8] *Id.*

[9] 14 CFR Part 91, Docket No. FAA-2006-25714, Department of Transportation, Federal Aviation Administration, Unmanned Aircraft Operations in the National Airspace System, February 6, 2007.

[10] *Unmanned Aerial Vehicles Support Border Security*, Customs and Border Protection Today, July 2004, www.cbp.gov/xp/CustomsToday/2004/Aug/other/aerial_vehicles.xml.

Border Patrol began operating a center in Cocoa Beach flying eight drones along Florida's shorelines and the Gulf Coast.[11]

Other documented non-military tasks have included earthquake damage assessment at Japan's Fukushima power plant, volcano activity assessment of Mount St. Helens in Washington for the U.S. Geological Survey, and surveying wild fires in Texas.[12]

At the University of Florida, over the last 12 years, the Unmanned Aerial Systems Research Group has been developing an 11 pound drone with a 9 foot wingspan that is called "Nova 2.1." According to researchers, it can be used to safely and accurately gather data that will be helpful to wildlife biologists and many others.[13]

Clearly, the drone industry is becoming motivated to move into more civilian markets.[14] Reportedly Florida is competing to secure a position as a leading development, testing, and manufacturing site for drones.[15]

Integrating Drones into the Nation's Airspace System

In February 2012 Congress passed the FAA Modernization and Reform Act of 2012 (Act), which requires the FAA to safely open the nation's airspace to drones by September 2015.[16] Under the timetable set forth by Congress, the FAA has authorized government public safety agencies to operate drones under certain restrictions and made the process for approving authorization requests more efficient.[17]

However, the FAA appears to be proceeding with caution in its implementation of the 2012 Federal Act. The FAA has delayed selecting the six test sites for drones mandated by Congress. Further, although it seems to be outside the congressional mandate and beyond the scope of the FAA's airspace-safety responsibilities, the FAA has notified Congress that "privacy issues" have become a concern as drones are integrated into the airspace.[18]

---

[11] *Space Florida Probing Drone's Future Potential,* Howard Altman, Tampa Bay Online, August 5, 2012, www2.tbo.com/news/breaking-news/2012/aug/05/space-florida-probing-drones-future-potential-ar-453511/.
[12] *Drones for Hire,* Air & Space Smithsonian, James Chiles, January 2013, www.airspacemag.com/flight-today/Drones-for-Hire-179517781.html.
[13] *Florida Hopes to Fill Its Skies with Unmanned Aircraft,* Florida Today, James Dean, June 23, 2012, http://usatoday30.usatoday.com/news/nation/story/2012-06-23/increased-drone-use-privacy-concerns/55783066/1; *UF Team's Work Pays Off With Unmanned-flight System that Captures Valuable Data,* Phys Org, October 20,2010, http://phys.org/news/2010-10-uf-team-unmanned-flight-captures-valuable.html.
[14] *Drones for Hire,* Air & Space Smithsonian, James Chiles, January 2013, www.airspacemag.com/flight-today/Drones-for-Hire-179517781.html.
[15] *Florida Vies to be America's Drone Capital,* RT, June 29, 2010, http://rt.com/usa/news/florida-drone-space-unmanned-091/print/.
[16] Public Law 112-95, February 14, 2012, The FAA Modernization and Reform Act of 2012; *Drones in Domestic Surveillance Operations,* Congressional Research Service, September 6, 2012, www.fas.org/sgp/crs/natsec/R42701.pdf.
[17] *FAA Makes Progress with UAS Integration,* Federal Aviation Administration, May 14, 2012, www.faa.gov/news/updates/?newsId=68004; Public Law 112-95, February 14, 2012, The FAA Modernization and Reform Act of 2012.
[18] A *Bloomberg* report quotes the FAA Acting Chief as having written to members of the Congressional Unmanned Systems Caucus: "However, increasing the use of UAS in our airspace also raises privacy issues, and these issues will need to be addressed as unmanned aircraft are safely integrated.". *FAA Going Slow on Drones as Privacy Concerns Studied,* Alan Levine, Bloomberg, November 26, 2012, http://go.bloomberg.com/political-capital/2012-11-26/faa-going-slow-.

Chapter 4

Administrative Law

I. Brief Overview of Administrative Lawmaking

Researching administrative law requires an understanding of the relationship among agencies, legislatures, courts, and the executive branch. This chapter, therefore, begins with an overview of the process of administrative lawmaking and then discusses specific sources for researching Florida and federal administrative law.

Agencies are created to regulate industries, professions, or practices that require close oversight and specialized expertise. Agencies also administer systems that require specialized fact-finding, such as the unemployment insurance system, workers' compensation system, or professional disciplinary systems.

The rules that agencies adopt to regulate the industry, profession, or practice with which they are charged are developed during a public rulemaking process. During this process agencies typically seek public comment, hold hearings, and review input from the public and the industry or profession to be regulated. In the federal system, these rules are referred to as "regulations," and most lawyers use the terms interchangeably. Once the rules are in place, agencies can adjudicate cases according to those rules. To do this, the agencies hold quasi-judicial hearings with pleadings, briefs, witnesses, arguments, and a written decision explaining the outcome, similar to actual judicial proceedings.

Agencies are created by legislative action. A statute creating an agency and defining its mission is called an "enabling statute." Enabling statutes set out the substantive law the agency is charged with applying and give the agency rulemaking authority in that area. Enabling statutes also impose limits on the power an agency may use in accomplishing its goals. In other words, agencies are created to meet specific goals and are given limited powers to help them accomplish those goals. Sometimes an existing agency is given charge of a new program.

In addition to creating agencies, the legislature can oversee agencies in a number of ways. Legislatures will sometimes hold oversight hearings to examine whether an agency is properly performing its job. Legislatures also control the funding of agencies, and a legislature may cut funding to an agency if it disagrees with the agency's action or wants to diminish its impact. The legislature can pass new statutory law in response to the agency's action, even eliminating the agency. Finally, in many jurisdictions the legislature must approve the executive's appointment of top agency officials. In Florida, the Joint Administrative Procedures Committee (JAPC), which includes members of both the Senate and the House of Representatives, is responsible for administrative agency oversight. The JAPC website, www.japc.state.fl.us, provides links to information about committee meetings and activities.

The executive branch plays an important role in agency administration, in that the executive typically appoints top agency officials. Depending on the jurisdiction and the agency, the executive might be able to appoint or remove an agency head at any time; alternatively, the executive may appoint an agency head but be limited to removing that official for cause. Some agency officials are elected, as well. The relationship is often reciprocal; the agency's top official may be part of the executive's cabinet or some other advisory group.

The judicial branch also has an important role in administrative law. The judiciary can review administrative action to determine whether the action was within the agency's power, as defined by the enabling statute. A court can also review whether the agency used the proper procedures in taking its action. Litigants who are unhappy with the result of quasi-judicial agency proceedings sometimes have a limited right of appeal to the courts, as well.

II. Researching Administrative Law Issues

Because of the relationship between agencies and other parts of government, research in administrative law often needs to be more comprehensive than simply finding an applicable rule. Administrative law research may include one or all of the following five goals: finding agency regulations; finding agency and judicial decisions interpreting the regulations; finding the agency's enabling statute; finding case law interpreting the enabling statute; and determining whether an agency acted within the relevant Administrative Procedures Act (APA). The five steps are summarized in Table 4-1. This part of the chapter describes the process in general terms; specific sources for locating Florida and federal administrative materials are described in Parts III and IV, below.

Table 4-1. Process for Researching Administrative Law

---

1. Find applicable regulations in an administrative code.

2. Read administrative and judicial decisions that interpret the regulation.

3. Find the enabling statute.

4. Read case law interpreting the enabling statute.

5. Review the applicable Administrative Procedure Act.

A. Finding Applicable Regulations

When working in state or federal administrative materials, the starting point is often the index to the appropriate regulatory code. Both print and online sources are available for searching in a variety of ways, as discussed in more detail below. Sometimes you will know when you begin your research that you are looking for regulations that relate to a particular enabling statute. The annotations to that statute or the case law interpreting that statute may provide a reference to related regulations. Once you have found the applicable regulation, you will typically need to check to see whether any changes to the text of the regulation have recently been proposed or approved.

B. Finding Administrative and Judicial Decisions Interpreting the Regulation

Although it is possible that your goal will simply be to find the text of an applicable regulation, you should verify that your regulation has not been challenged or invalidated. Some agencies have their own reporters for agency decisions. You may also find references to agency and court decisions in statutory annotations, secondary sources, and indexes. Practice area services[1] will also

---

1. Practice area services include specialized publications that gather the text of primary sources, library references, and commentary in a specific topical area. They tend to be published in areas of the law that are heavily regulated, and are often used by administrative law practitioners. Practice area services are discussed further in Chapter 7.

lead you to decisions interpreting regulations. You can Shepardize or KeyCite the regulation to find its direct history and related cases.

C. Finding the Enabling Statute

In both state and federal administrative law research, you can use a statutory index to find an enabling statute dealing with your subject matter, and then use that statute to locate applicable rules. If you are starting with no leads and little knowledge of the subject, it may be easier to use some other tools, such as secondary sources or practice area services, for your initial background research. These sources will often refer you to both statutory and regulatory authority. If you are starting with a cite to a particular rule, you can go directly to that source and check for references to the appropriate enabling statute. Note that a rule can refer to more than one statutory authority. Each rule in the *Florida Administrative Code* includes a history note giving the statutory authority for that rule and the statute that the rule implements (they are not always the same statute).

D. Finding Case Law Interpreting the Enabling Statute

After identifying the enabling statute, you can use annotated statutes or secondary sources to locate case law interpreting the statute, or use the enabling statute as a search term on Lexis or Westlaw. You can also update the enabling statute online using Shepard's or KeyCite to find other authorities citing the statute.

E. Reviewing an Administrative Procedure Act

All states and the federal government have procedural acts that set out general guidelines, limitations, and procedures for agencies to follow in carrying out their mission. In Florida, agency proceedings are subject to the Administrative Procedure Act in the Florida Statutes.[2] Federal agencies are similarly subject to the federal Administrative Procedure Act.[3] If your research involves finding out whether a particular agency used the proper procedures in reaching a decision or taking some regulatory action, you may need to look at the terms

---

2. *See* §§ 120.50-.81, Fla. Stat.
3. *See* 5 U.S.C. §§ 551–559.

of the applicable procedural act and related rules in addition to looking at that agency's unique rules.

III. Florida Administrative Law Research

Table 4-2 summarizes the sources used for administrative law research in Florida. An excellent starting point is the JAPC website, which includes a link for "Legal Research." The Florida Rules website at www.flrules.org also provides helpful background information from a link "What is the F.A.C.?"

Table 4-2. Florida Administrative Law Sources

Source	Contents
Florida Statutes	enabling statutes
Florida Statutes Annotated/ Florida Annotated Statutes	enabling statutes and annotations to cases interpreting them
Florida Administrative Code (FAC)	agency regulations
Florida Administrative Register (FAR)	proposed rules, rule changes, and related information
Florida Administrative Law Reports	agency decisions

A. *Florida Administrative Code*

The *Florida Administrative Code* (FAC) is the official administrative code for Florida and is published online by the Department of State at www.flrules.org. The FAC is also available on Westlaw. LexisNexis publishes the *Florida Administrative Code Annotated*, available in print and on Lexis, which provides the text of the rules and identifies court and agency decisions applying the rules.

The FAC is organized by title numbers and subtitle letters. Each agency has a designated title number for its regulations. The subtitle letter, if any, represents a division within the agency. Within each subtitle are chapters, which contain all the rules relating to a specific subject. For example, the Florida Department of Financial Services, which oversees a number of different programs, has its regulations in Title 69. The Division of Workers' Compensation, which is part of that Department, has its regulations in Title 69L. That title includes a number of chapters, including 69L-3, Workers' Compensation

Claims; 69L-5, Rules for Self-Insurers Under the Workers' Compensation Act; and 69L-24, Insurers' Standards and Practices. Each of those chapters, finally, contains a number of specific rules relating to the subject of the chapter. A citation to Rule 69L-3.002, then, would take you to a specific rule within Chapter 3 of Title 69L.

At the end of each rule in the FAC, a history note tells when the rule has been modified, renumbered, or repealed. The history note also gives the relevant enabling section of Florida Statutes. This information is essential if you are trying to track the development of a rule, or if you need to verify that the current version of the rule was in effect when your research situation occurred. An example of a rule and history note appears in Table 4-3.

Table 4-3. Example of a Rule in the *Florida Administrative Code*

34-6.001 General

The Commission on Ethics is authorized to render advisory opinions about the application of the Sunshine Amendment (Article II, Section 8, Florida Constitution), of the Code of Ethics for Public Officers and Employees (Part III, Chapter 112, Florida Statutes), and of Sections 350.031, 350.04, 350.041, and 350.042, Florida Statutes. If a person does not have standing to receive an advisory opinion from the Commission, but would have standing to receive a declaratory statement, or if the Commission does not have the authority to render an advisory opinion, but would have the authority to render a declaratory statement, the Commission may issue a declaratory statement.

Rulemaking Authority 112.322(9) FS. Law Implemented 112.3215(10), 112.322(3), 350.041(3), 350.043 FS. History–New 4-11-76, Amended 9-21-77, Formerly 34-6.01, Amended 8-7-94, 7-28-98.

Source: Florida Department of State, www.flrules.org.

The FAC also includes a set of uniform rules of procedure, adopted pursuant to section 120.545 of the Florida APA, to be used in agency proceedings. These rules are found in FAC Chapters 28-101 through 28-112.

1. FAC Online

The electronic version of the FAC at www.flrules.org is the official version, and it is available for free. Therefore, it should be the preferred source for Florida administrative rules. In addition to key word searching, the site allows you to go directly to specific titles, chapters, or divisions; you can also search

Figure 4-1. FAC Online

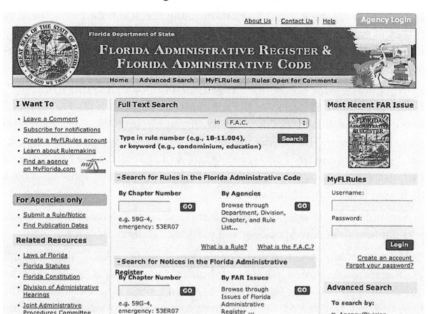

Source: Florida Department of State, www.flrules.org.

by going directly to a specific agency or department and looking at the rules that agency has promulgated.[4]

Your search results on the Florida Rules website will include information on proposed and pending action affecting the title or chapter you are researching, which facilitates updating. A link will take you to the text of the rule you retrieved. An example of the information provided in the FAC online appears in Figure 4-1.

Westlaw and Lexis have administrative rules databases that are updated frequently. But for the most current version of a rule, rely on the Florida Rules website.

---

4. A small disadvantage of the current site is that, to look at the text of specific rules, you must retrieve one rule at a time; you cannot easily browse entire chapters as would be possible in the print version or using Westlaw or Lexis. However, you can still browse the contents for each chapter and division, and doing that is strongly encouraged when you are using the online version — don't stop with a single applicable rule without reading other rules in the same chapter.

2. FAC in Print

The FAC is a looseleaf publication, meaning that it is published in binders that allow specific pages to be replaced when rules change rather than reprinting the entire publication. The binders are updated monthly by inserting replacement pages.

When you already have a rule citation, simply look up the rule in the FAC. If you do not have a citation to the relevant rule, begin with the FAC General Index, which is stored in its own binder. If you cannot find a specific rule on point in the General Index, identify the title or titles that appear to be relevant. Go directly to those titles and scan the tables of contents at the beginning of each title for specific rules. In addition to tables of contents, some titles have their own indexes at the end of the title.

The index binder also contains a "Statutory Cross Reference Table" where you can find rules corresponding to a particular statute.

If the index leads you to a specific rule, you should check the "Repealed and Transferred Table," stored in a separate binder.[5] Often a rule is still listed under one number in the index long after it has been given a different number; the Repealed and Transferred Table will list a history note for each rule that has been either repealed or renumbered, so that you can quickly find the "new" location of the rule.

B. *Florida Administrative Register*

The *Florida Administrative Register* (FAR), formerly known as *Florida Administrative Weekly* (FAW), is a daily online publication that includes information about administrative rules, including proposed rules and proposed changes to existing rules. In addition to rules, the FAR publishes information about state agencies, requests for bids on agency contracts, and similar information. The FAR is available only online at the Florida Rules website www.flrules.org and is no longer published in print. Full-text searching is available in the electronic version. FAR is not currently available on WestlawNext or Lexis, but Lexis provides access to FAW issues from 1996 until 2012.

---

5. Sometimes entire titles are moved to a new number. This can happen, for example, when agencies are reorganized or their responsibilities are altered by the legislature. In the workers' compensation example at the beginning of this chapter, those rules were previously part of Title 38F, when workers' compensation was administered by the Department of Labor and Employment Security. They were transferred to the new title in 2005.

C. Updating a Rule

The FAC is part of the Shepard's and KeyCite services,[6] and updating a rule with either service will provide citing references including judicial and administrative decisions citing the rule, along with information on proposed amendments to the rule. However, the coverage in Shepard's and KeyCite is not identical, so you should use both services whenever possible. Additionally, the Florida Rules website, www.flrules.org, allows searches by rule number in the FAC and the FAR, which may provide additional information on recent changes or proposed changes.

D. Historical Research

Sometimes a research project will require more than simply finding a current rule. For example, you might need to investigate changes to a rule that were proposed, but not adopted, in a previous year. You can do a full-text search of both the FAC and FAR at www.flrules.org dating back to January 1, 2006. To do further research, you will need to browse *List of Rules Affected* in older issues of the FAW. Because the lists and indexes in FAW are not cumulative, you will have to repeat the process for each volume of FAW that covers the period relevant to your project. The Florida Rules website currently has issues of FAW dating back to 1999.

You might also need to find the previous text of a rule that has been changed. In litigation you must use the regulation that was in effect when your case arose, which may not be the same as the current regulation. Looking at the current version of the rule, you can determine when it was amended. Depending on the dates involved, you might be able to find the previous version through the Florida Rules website. However, older pages from the FAC itself are not currently available through the Florida Rules website. Some law libraries keep outdated pages from the FAC in an archive. Further, each agency is required to keep its own old rules, so if you need copies of an old rule, you may have to call or write to the agency.

E. Decisions of Administrative Agencies

Because FAC annotations include few cases, you will have to use other methods to find administrative and judicial interpretations of relevant rules. One of the main sources for agency decisions is *Florida Administrative Law Reports* (FALR).

FALR publishes selected administrative law opinions from some agencies and is the official reporter for most other agencies. Some of the agencies covered

---

6. These citators are covered in Chapter 5.

are listed in Table 4-4; a complete list of agencies whose decisions are included in FALR appears at the beginning of each FALR volume or can be found online. (Because FALR is published by a commercial publisher, the full text of the online version is only available by subscription.) For the covered agencies, most but not all of the agencies' decisions are reported in FALR. FALR also publishes judicial opinions involving administrative law. These judicial decisions should be cited to the *Southern Reporter* if they appear in that series.

Table 4-4. Selected Agencies Covered in FALR

Agency for Health Care Administration

Medical Quality Assurance Boards

Department of Children and Families

Department of Health

Department of Environmental Protection

Education Practices Commission

Ethics Commission

Department of Highway Safety and Motor Vehicles

Department of Revenue

Department of Agriculture and Consumer Services (Division of Licensing)

Department of Education

Department of Juvenile Justice

* A full list is available at http://www.falr.com/agencies.shtml.

There are many indexes to FALR, and using them requires close attention to dates. Each volume has its own index. One of the very helpful features of the print FALR indexes is the Table of Administrative Rules Construed, telling you which decisions refer to specific rules.[7] Cumulative indexes covering periods of one or several years are also available. Not all libraries purchase the same indexes, however. Pay close attention to the dates covered by the index you are using, and don't hesitate to ask a reference librarian for assistance.

The FALR website provides access to several cumulative indexes covering different time periods. The indexes can be searched free of charge, but then

---

7. This table is actually an internal "citator"; it provides information similar to what you would find if you were to Shepardize or KeyCite a Florida rule.

you must pay a fee for retrieving the cases referenced there (the website does not provide the FALR citation, but instead provides a reference number that FALR staff can use to retrieve the desired decision).

In addition to the general edition of FALR, specialized editions of FALR deal with environmental law and tax law. The special reporters for FALR do not necessarily include the same opinions as the general FALR; in other words, they are not merely a subset of the information that appears in the general FALR. Two other series from the same publisher are the *Florida Public Service Commission Reporter* and the *Florida Career Service Reporter*.

Many agencies are not covered by FALR, or their decisions are only partially covered. To find their decisions, you may have to contact the agency and ask for a copy of the subject index for that agency's decisions. The Florida Administrative Procedure Act (APA) requires each agency to keep a subject index of all of its decisions. Because the process of finding Florida administrative decisions may be time consuming and frustrating, it may be easier to use a topical practice area service, as mentioned in footnote 1.

If the agency you are researching is one of the many agencies that use the Division of Administrative Hearings (DOAH) for its hearings, rather than holding them internally, you can use the DOAH website, www.doah.state.fl.us, to research final orders in relevant cases. Be careful to make the distinction between recommended orders and final orders. DOAH provides administrative law judges to hear cases involving the violation or application of administrative rules in a number of areas. The Agency for Health Care Regulation, the Department of Revenue, the Department of Business and Professional Regulation, and the Department of Health are just a few of the Florida agencies that use DOAH. So, for example, if you were interested in the regulations governing the profession of nursing and wanted to locate recent decisions involving disciplinary actions against licensed nurses, you could search for those types of decisions through the DOAH website. DOAH also provides Judges of Compensation Claims to hear workers' compensation cases. Their decisions can be searched at the website of the Office of the Judges of Compensation Claims, www.jcc.state.fl.us/jcc.

WestlawNext includes several specialized administrative databases. Browsing under "State Materials," click on "Florida," then "Florida Administrative Decisions & Guidance," and you will find DOAH decisions, Office of the Judges of Compensation Claims Decisions, Public Service Commission Decisions, and Environmental Administrative Decisions, for example. Using "Browse Sources" in Lexis Advance, and typing "Florida" in the search box, you can find helpful databases such as Florida Workers' Compensation Decisions (which has selected opinions) and Florida Environmental and Land Use Decisions.

F. Attorney General Opinions

In many jurisdictions, including Florida, the state Attorney General is authorized by law to provide advisory opinions to state agencies regarding the effect of a particular state law. The Attorney General can also provide advisory opinions to members of the state legislature, Florida members of Congress, and various state officers. While these opinions are non-binding, they can be highly persuasive. They are potentially helpful when researching agency actions because some of them are written in response to a query from an agency about how a particular statute will affect that agency.

The Attorney General's website, www.myfloridalegal.com, has a searchable database of Attorney General opinions dating back to approximately 1974. Examples of opinions include:

- an opinion requested by the city attorney of Deltona, Florida, regarding the application of a section of Florida Statutes governing contracts for professional services between a municipality and a service provider;

- an opinion requested by a city commission regarding whether emails sent by city commissioners that contain undisclosed recipients and their email addresses are public records subject to disclosure under Florida's public records laws; and

- an opinion requested by the Sheriff of Santa Rosa County regarding the confidentiality of certain information in a juvenile's misdemeanor file.

All Florida Attorney General opinions are also searchable on Lexis. Westlaw has coverage beginning in 1977.

IV. Federal Administrative Law Materials

The sources for federal administrative law materials parallel those used for Florida research. Table 4-5 summarizes the sources that are most often used.

Table 4-5. Federal Administrative Law Sources

Source	Contents
United States Code	enabling statutes
United States Code Annotated/ United States Code Service	enabling statutes and annotations to cases interpreting them
Code of Federal Regulations (CFR)	agency regulations
Federal Register	proposed agency action and related information
List of Sections Affected (LSA)	tables of rule changes

One source that is often helpful at the beginning stages of federal research is the *United States Government Manual*, which is an annual directory of the federal government with an emphasis on the executive branch and regulatory agencies. It is available online at www.usgovernmentmanual.gov. Each executive department and federal agency is listed with the following information: (1) citation to the enabling statute creating that department or agency; (2) agency descriptions of function and authority; (3) a list of subsidiary units and predecessor agencies; (4) the names and functions of the major officials; (5) organizational charts; and (6) sources of information available from the agency. When using annotated codes, note that *United States Code Service* (USCS) provides more references to regulations than *United States Code Annotated* (USCA), so you might start researching administrative law in USCS.[8]

A. *Code of Federal Regulations*

The *Code of Federal Regulations* (CFR) is a compilation of all federal regulations arranged by subject matter. Each volume of CFR contains an alphabetical list of all federal agencies with their titles and chapters. CFR is divided into 50 titles. While some title numbers are the same as in the *United States Code* (USC), the titles do not necessarily correspond to each other.[9] Each title of CFR is divided into chapters. Each chapter contains all the regulations from a specific agency. Each chapter is divided into parts. A part contains all the regulations from an agency on a particular topic. Each part includes an au-

---

8. These annotated versions of the *United States Code* are discussed in Chapter 3.
9. As an example, Title 26 in both CFR and USC concerns Internal Revenue.

thority note that cites the statute giving the agency authority to create the regulations contained in the part. Each part (or sometimes individual sections) also includes a source note, which cites the page of the *Federal Register* where the regulation was last published in full.

The CFR can be searched on the Government Printing Office's[10] Federal Digital System, "FDsys," at www.gpoaccess.gov/fdsys, which is relatively simple to use. It allows you to go directly to a specific regulation, to browse the contents of each title, or to locate applicable provisions using key word searching. It also provides access to previous versions of the CFR, going back to 1996. It is updated on the same schedule as the print version. However, the GPO also publishes an unofficial electronic version of the CFR on FDsys. Click on the tab for "Code of Federal Regulations" and then "Electronic Code of Federal Regulations" (e-CFR). The unofficial version is updated daily and is a good source for making sure you have the most recent text of an applicable regulation, although you would still need to verify your information in official sources.

Individual agency sites also often include links to the regulations promulgated by that agency and, if you already know the agency in question, can be a speedy way to locate applicable regulations. Using WestlawNext, you can click on "Federal Materials," then "Code of Federal Regulations." You will then see a table of contents, which can be expanded to include more detail, and a link to the index. Also included is a link to "CFR Historical," which provides access to versions of the CFR beginning in 1984. On Lexis Advance, go to "Browse Sources," and search for "Code of Federal Regulations." There you will be able to view the table of contents and obtain links directly to regulations, or choose to add CFR to your search for full-text searching. Lexis Advance provides access to the current CFR, but as of this printing, the CFR archives are available only on Lexis.com, going back to 1981.

B. *Federal Register*

The *Federal Register*, published every weekday, lists recent agency actions or proposed actions. The *Federal Register* also publishes changes in federal regulations.[11] For a new regulation, the *Federal Register* prints the regulation when

---

10. The name is being changed to Government Publishing Office.
11. A federal website, www.regulations.gov, provides links to proposed regulations and agency action, and allows users to submit comments through the website. Although it does not replace official sources, it is another gateway to information about current administrative law developments.

it is proposed and open for public comment, and reprints it when it is adopted. While CFR gives the text of regulations that were current when that volume of CFR was published, it is necessary to use the *Federal Register* to research the history of a regulation and to update regulations in the CFR. The *Federal Register* also includes information that is not found in CFR, such as descriptions of agency organization and reorganization, a policy statement about each new rule, and rules that have been repealed.

The *Federal Register* is available online through FDsys as well as Lexis and Westlaw. FDsys, at www.gpoaccess.gov/fdsys, allows both simple and more advanced searching and browsing of the volumes for the current year, and also provides access to former issues dating back to 1994. WestlawNext provides full-text searching of issues going back to 1981 and has PDF versions of even older issues, going back to 1936. On Lexis Advance, you can search the current version in "Federal Register" or search issues all the way back to 1936 using "Federal Register All."

C. Researching Changes in a Federal Regulation

1. FDsys

To find changes in a regulation that have occurred since the regulation was last published in CFR, go to FDsys and search the *List of Sections Affected* (LSA). The LSA, published monthly, is a list of sections of regulations that were changed during that month and all preceding months since the CFR was last updated. The LSA is cumulative, and the website contains issues of the LSA beginning in 1997. Start by looking in LSA to find the title and section number of the regulation that you want to update. If you do not find your section listed, it has not been changed during the time period covered by the LSA. If you find your section listed, you will see a citation next to the section. This citation is a page number in the *Federal Register*. Go to that page of the *Federal Register* to find the change in your regulation.

After checking the LSA and the cited pages in the *Federal Register*, you must update your research even further by using a "List of Parts Affected" in the *Federal Register*. Information in LSA is a few months behind the *Federal Register*. For example, you might find that on July 5 the most recent LSA was for April 28. You would have to continue to update your regulation from April 28 through July 5. On the LSA page at FDsys, you will find a link that allows you to "Browse CFR Parts Affected from the Federal Register." You can limit the search to the last 24 hours, last week, or last month, or you can specify a date range for the search.

2. Shepard's and KeyCite

Federal regulations can be updated using Shepard's or KeyCite. As with annotated statutes, your search results may include legislative and judicial actions that affect a particular regulation. Pay close attention to any notations indicating that your regulation has been held constitutional or unconstitutional (in whole or in part), or that it has been voided or invalidated.

D. Finding Old Regulations

Older versions of CFR are important because litigation often occurs long after the incident that is the subject of the litigation. You may have a case involving a building that was constructed in 1990. The litigation may include allegations of a construction defect. A partial defense may be that the builder complied with all safety regulations of the Occupational Safety and Health Administration in effect at that time. You could not answer this question using a current CFR. You would have to look at the CFR volume for the time the building was constructed — 1990.

As online coverage of federal administrative sources has increased, it has become easier to do this type of research. However, it is still possible that you may need to consult a volume that predates current online coverage. Many larger law libraries keep old issues of CFR, either in paper form or on microfiche.

As described above, the *Federal Register* and LSA can also be used to trace historical changes in a particular regulation or set of regulations.

E. Decisions of Administrative Agencies

Some federal agencies publish their own reporters for agency decisions. Other agency decisions are covered by unofficial reporters. An agency's website will often provide information about where to find that agency's decisions. If you cannot find a reporter for a federal agency's decisions, consult a topical practice area service or other secondary source. Lexis and Westlaw both have administrative law databases containing federal agency decisions.

F. Attorney General Opinions

The United States Attorney General is the chief law enforcement officer of the federal government and serves as the head of the Department of Justice. Unlike most state Attorneys General, the United States Attorney General is appointed to the office. As in state government, however, one of the functions of the Department of Justice is to provide legal advice and opinions to various federal agencies. This responsibility has been delegated to the Office of Legal Counsel, which, since 1977, has published advisory opinions in *Opinions of the Office of Legal Counsel*. Although advisory opinions are not binding, they can be used as persuasive authority when analyzing federal statutes or agency action. Advisory opinions are also available through the Department of Justice website, www.justice.gov/olc/opinions.htm, and on both Westlaw and Lexis. On WestlawNext, go to the "Federal Materials" tab, click on "Federal Administrative Decisions & Guidance," then on "Department of Justice," and you will find U.S. Attorney General Opinions. On Lexis Advance, go to "Browse Sources," type in "U.S. Attorney General Opinions," then "Add This Source to the Search."

Chapter 5

Updating

Updating the legal authorities you find in the research process is important for two reasons: to validate the currency of each authority and to use relevant authorities to locate additional authorities.

First, to use any legal authority to analyze a problem, you must know how that authority has been treated by later actions of a court, legislature, or agency. For example, a case may have been reversed or overruled; a statute may have been amended or repealed. Ensuring that the cases, statutes, and other authorities you rely on represent the current law is a critical step in the research process.

To update an authority, you must find every subsequent legal source that has cited your authority and determine how the subsequent source treated your authority on a particular issue. To begin, you need a list of citations to sources that refer to your authority. A *citator* provides that list. Online citators provide the most efficient way to update authorities, and most online sources of legal material provide a citator.[1]

The second reason for updating is related to the first: a list of authorities that have cited your case or statute will likely include additional sources that are relevant to your research. Thus, updating one case or statute can lead you to many other cases, court documents, and secondary sources that are also relevant to your work.

The most sophisticated citators are provided by Lexis and Westlaw.[2] Lexis provides the "Shepard's" online citator; Westlaw provides a citator called

---

1. Updating can be performed with books called *Shepard's Citations*. However, the process is complicated and few libraries maintain current copies of the books needed to update sources comprehensively. If you ever need to update with *Shepard's Citations*, seek the services of a law reference librarian or follow the meticulous instructions in the front of any volume.

2. Table 1-1 in Chapter 1 of this book lists the citators for a number of online services. Bloomberg includes a citator called BCite, which is quite good. Citators provided

"KeyCite." Coverage between Shepard's and KeyCite is not completely identical, and new material is constantly being added to each. Still, for determining whether a case or another primary authority is valid and for expanding your research, the services can be used interchangeably.

Using these services to update an authority is easy; for each service, you simply type a citation in the appropriate box or click on an updating icon or tab while viewing the document. Understanding the search results can be difficult at first, but it becomes second nature with practice. Even so, updating is almost always a time-consuming activity, primarily because of the number of sources you must read and analyze. But thorough research requires updating, and your research is not finished until this step has been completed for each authority that you use in your legal analysis. Moreover, the possibility of finding additional authorities relevant to your research makes updating a smart step early in the research process.

I. The Updating Process

The process of updating an authority refers frequently to two basic, and possibly confusing, terms: the cited source and the citing sources. The authority you are updating is the *cited source*. Throughout this chapter, a Florida case will be used as the example of a cited source.[3] The authorities listed in a citator that refer to your case are called *citing sources* (or sometimes *citing references* or *citing decisions*). Although the terminology is very similar, for each updating search there is only one cited source while there may be many citing sources.

The process of updating includes finding all the subsequent sources that cite your case, analyzing the symbols provided by the citator, and reading and analyzing the citing sources to determine their impact on your case and their relevance to your research. This process is summarized in Table 5-1.

---

by other online services tend to be less robust. They are helpful as an initial approach to updating, or for expanding research, but should not be relied on to validate authorities.

3. As discussed below, a variety of sources can be Shepardized or KeyCited. However, these services are perhaps most helpful for updating cases and statutes, and so a case example is used here.

Table 5-1. Outline for Updating Online

___

1. Access the citator either by entering your citation in the box provided or by clicking on the updating icon or tab while you are viewing the document.

2. Select the type of citation list you need:

   • a short list showing the direct history and/or negative treatment of the cited source,

   • a longer list showing all subsequent sources that cite your authority, or

   • a list of the cases that your case has cited (called the "Table of Authorities").

3. Analyze the analytical symbols provided by the citator. Consider limiting your citator results by jurisdiction, headnote, date, or other parameter.

4. Prioritize and read the citing sources. Analyze the impact, if any, these sources have on the authority you are updating. Even if the sources have no impact on the authority you are updating, determine whether they provide additional support for your analysis.

___

The fourth step is the same regardless of which citator you use: reading the cases and other citing references. While a citator can alert you to possible problems, only you can decide the impact of an authority on the case you want to use in your analysis. Reading these authorities is easy online. Clicking on the name of a source in the citator list will take you either (a) to the first page of the citing source, where you will be able to click on "Search Term" to go to the page where your authority is cited or (b) immediately to the point in the citing source where your case is cited. You can quickly skim the relevant portion of the citing source and decide whether it is relevant to your research.

In reading the citing sources, decide whether they address the legal question at issue in your client's problem. If a source analyzes only points of your case that are not relevant to your client's situation, disregard that source. If a source is on point, analyze its impact on your case: Does this new source change the rule announced in your case, either by reversing or overruling it? Or does it follow your case by simply restating the rule and applying it to a similar fact pattern? Does the new source distinguish or criticize your case? If so, why and how? Be wary of any criticism of your authorities — opposing counsel will be quick to point it out to your judge.

A. KeyCite on WestlawNext[4]

1. Access the Citator

On WestlawNext, you can go directly to KeyCite information by typing either "kc:" or "keycite" and then the case citation. See Figure 5-1. Additionally, a set of KeyCite tabs appears whenever you open a case (or other document) that is included in the KeyCite service. See Figure 5-2. At the top of the document page, you will see an icon showing whether Westlaw considers the case to be good law, along with the most recent negative treatment of the case, if any.

2. Select the Citation List Needed

The tab "Negative Treatment" contains the most harmful of the sources that have cited your case. Here you will learn whether your case has been reversed, overruled, distinguished, etc. The "History" tab lists other decisions during your case's litigation, including orders being affirmed, reversed, or remanded, as well as certiorari being denied. This information is available both in list and

Figure 5-1. KeyCiting a Case on WestlawNext

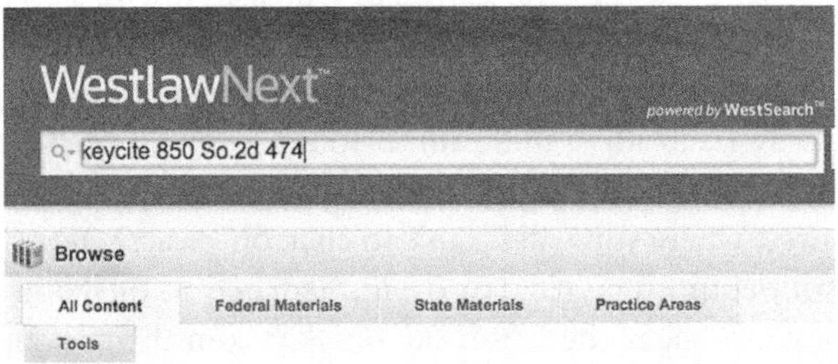

Source: WestlawNext. Reprinted with permission of Thomson Reuters.

---

4. Using KeyCite on Westlaw Classic is quite similar. You access the citator through a "KEYCITE" link at the top of the search screen, by typing a citation into the KeyCite box in the left frame, or by clicking on a KeyCite symbol for a document you are viewing. The two lists of citing references include "Full History" and "Citing References," with the latter being the more comprehensive. You can limit the KeyCite search results by jurisdiction, date, headnote, etc., using the "Limit KeyCite Display" button.

Figure 5-2. KeyCite Tabs on WestlawNext

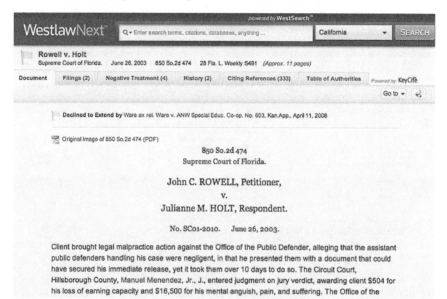

Source: WestlawNext. Reprinted with permission of Thomson Reuters.

graphic form. The tab "Citing References" contains all of the documents that have cited your case, meaning that it duplicates the other tabs and adds sources that are not negative or history. The final tab, "Table of Authorities," lists all of the cases cited by the case you are updating. This tab is useful in part because it provides a convenient way to see whether you have read all of the authorities cited by a case you know is relevant. More significantly, this tab can help you discover hidden weaknesses in your case: if a case it relied on heavily has been reversed, your case might be on shaky ground.

3. Analyze Results and Filter

The results list for Citing References (see Figure 5-3) labels the sources providing the most negative treatment. You can sort results by depth of treatment or by date, using a drop-down menu. You can also decide how much detail about the case you want to appear just under the title; click on the icon showing one, two, or three horizontal lines. The results list shows the depth of treatment each source gives your case, using one to four green bars to show how extensively a source has discussed your case. Finally, the results list indicates which

Figure 5-3. WestlawNext Citing References with Filters

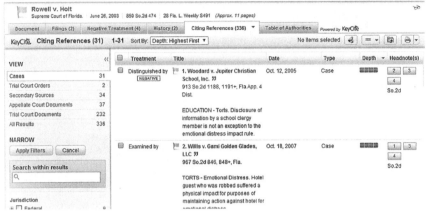

Source: WestlawNext. Reprinted with permission of Thomson Reuters.

headnote of your case is addressed in the citing source; holding your cursor over a headnote will allow you to review that headnote and determine whether it is relevant to your research.

The number of results under the Citing References tab can reach into the hundreds or thousands. Use the filters in the left margin to concentrate on the sources most likely to be helpful. You can limit the results to just cases, secondary sources, or court documents that cite your case. Then you can narrow by word, jurisdiction, date, depth of treatment, headnote, etc. Figure 5-3 shows some of the filters available for cases under the Citing References tab. Remember that you are filtering the results to know which citing sources deserve most of your attention; read these sources carefully.

B. Shepard's on Lexis Advance

1. Access the Citator

Shepard's may be accessed in several ways on Lexis Advance. When you are viewing a document, click on the "Shepardize" link at the top of the page or the citator symbol next to the case name (e.g., a yellow triangle or a red stop sign). Otherwise, to open a Shepard's report, type the citation into the main search bar and click on the "Shepard's" link just below and to the right. The resulting Shepard's tab is easily identified by the red "S" icon on the left. See Figure 5-4.

Figure 5-4. Shepard's on Lexis Advance

⬜ Rowell v. Holt, 85... ❌	⑤ Rowell v. Holt, 85... ❌	Terms & Conditio

Appellate History (4)	⚠ Citing Decisions (33)	Citing Law Reviews, Treatises... (95)	Table of Authorities

Shepard's®: ⚠ Rowell v. Holt, 850 So. 2d 474, 2003 Fla. LEXIS 1070, 28 Fla. L. Weekly S 491(Fla.,2003)

📄 List	⬀ Map	No subsequent appellate history. Prior history available.

🖨 💾 🗂 📋 📄   ⇐ 1 - 4 of 4 ⇒   📋 Legend

🗂 Appellate History	Court	Date
Prior		
1. Holt v. Rowell ⓐ	Fla. Dist. Ct. App. 2d Dist.	2000
758 So. 2d 677, 2000 Fla. App. LEXIS 6345		
Show on Map		
2. Related proceeding at:	Fla. Dist. Ct. App. 2d Dist.	2001
Holt v. Rowell ⬤		
798 So. 2d 767, 2001 Fla. App. LEXIS 11854, 26 Fla. L. Weekly D 2028		
Show on Map		
3. Review or Rehearing granted by:	Fla.	2002
Rowell v. Holt ⓐ		
816 So. 2d 129, 2002 Fla. LEXIS 492		
Show on Map		
4. ⭐ Citation you Shepardized™	Fla.	2003
Approved by ,		
in part ,		
Quashed by ,		
in part and		
Remanded by:		
Rowell v. Holt ⚠ 🔍		
850 So. 2d 474, 2003 Fla. LEXIS 1070, 28 Fla. L. Weekly S 491		
Show on Map		

Source: Reprinted with permission of Lexis Advance.

2. Select the Type of Citing List

Shepard's offers four tabs for validating your case and expanding your research. "Appellate History" provides any prior and subsequent history for your case, as shown in part in Figure 5-4. This information is available either in a list or in a map. "Citing Decisions" lists all of the cases that have cited your case, both in list form and in a variety of grids. The grids show the number of cases that have analyzed your case in the same way (e.g., questioned) over time. The third tab's full name is "Citing Law Reviews, Treatises, Annotated Statutes, Court Documents, Restatements, and other Secondary Sources," although not all of that appears on the tab. The last tab is the "Table of Authorities," listing the sources that your case cited.

3. Analyze the Citator Symbols and Limit the Search Results

Figure 5-5 shows the list of citing decisions for a Florida case. You can determine the order in which these cases are listed using the "Sort by" drop-down menu: court, date, depth of discussion, and type of analysis. Shepard's provides each of those four pieces of data for each case. A colored block accompanies the analysis description. Generally, red indicates a warning, orange and yellow suggest questioning or caution, green is positive, and blue is neutral. The "Legend" link on the right of the screen explains each symbol. See Figure 5-6 for an excerpt.

Next to the colored block and analysis description appears the name of the case. You can determine whether to receive just the case name, cite, and headnotes (clicking on "List") or to receive a short excerpt from the cited case (clicking "Detail"). The blue bars under "Discussion" show how much space the citing decision devoted to the case you are updating. For depth of discussion, four bars shows that the citing source analyzed your case, three bars shows discussion, two bars means that your case was mentioned, and one bar suggests your case was merely cited. The last two pieces of information provided are the court and date of decision.

Figure 5-5. Shepard's Citing Decisions

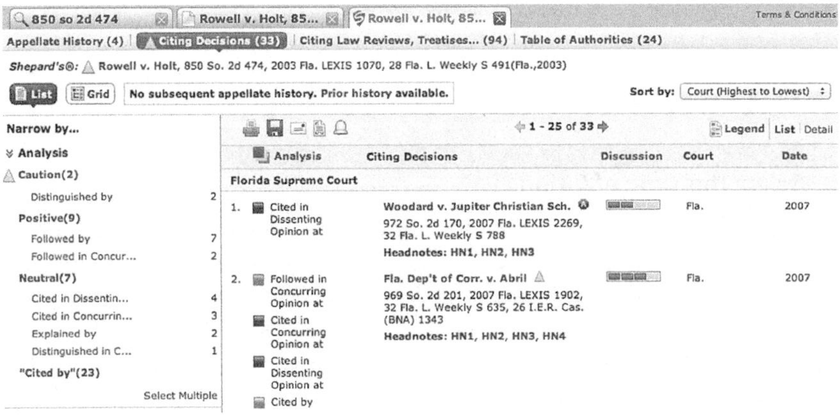

Source: Reprinted with permission of Lexis Advance.

Figure 5-6. Shepard's Legend

Legend

● Warning: Negative treatment is indicated

The red *Shepard's* Signal™ indicator indicates that citing references in the *Shepard's®* Citations Service contain strong negative history or treatment of your case (for example, overruled by or reversed).

(!) Warning: Negative treatment is indicated for statute

The red *Shepard's* Signal™ indicator indicates that citing references in the *Shepard's®* Citations Service contain strong negative treatment of the section (for example, the section may have been found to be unconstitutional or void).

[Q] Questioned: Validity questioned by citing reference.

The orange *Shepard's* Signal™ indicator indicates that the citing references in the *Shepard's®* Citations Service contain treatment that questions the continuing validity or precedential value of your case because of intervening circumstances, including judicial or legislative overruling

⚠ Caution: Possible negative treatment indicated

The yellow *Shepard's* Signal™ indicator indicates that citing references in the *Shepard's®* Citations Service contain history or treatment that may have a significant negative impact on your case (for example, limited or criticized by).

◆ Positive treatment indicated

The green *Shepard's* Signal™ indicator indicates that citing references in the *Shepard's®* Citations Service contain history or treatment that has a positive impact on your case (for example, affirmed or followed by).

Source: Reprinted with permission of Lexis Advance.

When faced with numerous results for citing decisions, concentrate your efforts on the most helpful by using filters in the left margin. As a few examples of narrowing citing decisions, you can restrict the list based on how each case analyzed the case you are Shepardizing (e.g., distinguished, followed, explained); the court that decided the citing cases; the depth of discussion (from one to four bars); Lexis headnotes in your case; word; and timeline. Under the "Secondary Sources ..." tab, you can narrow by content (court documents, treatises, law reviews, etc.), term, and timeline.

Clicking the hyperlinked name of a citing source will take you to that source, as will clicking the excerpt provided below the case name. To go directly to the point of the citing source that mentions the case you are updating, click on the pinpoint page (you will need to select "Detail" to have the pinpoint page available in the list of citing sources). Clicking on the Shepard's symbol at the end of the source's citation will take you to the Shepard's list for that case. As with KeyCite, it is important not to confuse these symbols with the symbol for the case you are updating. The more useful symbol is the one at the top of the page that gives the Shepard's view of your case.

C. Effective Use of Online Updating Tools

1. Colored Symbols

Some researchers give the colored symbols provided by KeyCite and Shepard's more weight than they deserve. A red symbol may simply mean that a lower court in another jurisdiction disagreed with the analysis of the case you are updating. That citing source has no impact on the weight of your case, but the red warns some researchers away. Similarly, the absence of that symbol may provide more comfort than is warranted. For example, sometimes a case becomes outdated without ever being specifically overruled. Unless another court overrules that decision, however, a citator will not warn you that the law may have changed. Be sure to read the citing references and decide for yourself whether your case is still good law.

2. Placement of Symbols

The placement of the colored symbols is important. A symbol next to a citing source—before the source on KeyCite and after the source on Shepard's—refers to that source, not to the cited source. In updating *Rowell v. Holt*, the case in Figure 5-5, you will see that one of its citing references, *Florida Department of Corrections v. Abril*, is followed by a yellow triangle. That symbol is a cautionary note about the treatment *Abril* has received, and clicking on it produces the Shepard's report for *Abril*. However, the green and blue boxes under the heading "Analysis" show that *Abril* has given *Rowell* positive and neutral treatment.

Note, too, that a source can give both positive and negative treatment to the cited case. This contradictory analysis occurs, for example, when a later case upholds one part of the cited case and overrules another.[5]

---

5. This situation arises when Shepardizing the case *United States v. Lee*, 22 F.3d 736 (7th Cir. 1994). Under the link for "Citing References," you will see the case *United States v. Howze* with both a red block showing that it overruled part of *Lee* and a green block showing that it followed another part of *Lee*. To illustrate the earlier point, the *Howze* case is followed by a yellow triangle, showing that it has received cautionary treatment from subsequent cases.

3. Headnote References

Both KeyCite and Shepard's indicate the headnotes from your cited case that are at least mentioned in the citing decision. You must remember, though, that the headnote numbers are not constant from one case to another. Returning to the example of *Rowell v. Holt*, assume that you know that Lexis headnote four is the only headnote relevant to your research project. You filter the Shepard's citing decisions by that headnote, resulting in six cases. Each citing decision will have a headnote that summarizes the same point of law summarized in headnote four of *Rowell*; however, that corresponding headnote in the citing source will probably have some number other than four. To illustrate, the *Abril* decision is one of the cases citing to the point of law in headnote four, but in *Abril*, the point of law is described under headnote eleven. That is, while headnotes in the cited source and the citing sources will address the same point of law, they will not match up number for number.

4. Prioritizing Citing References

After obtaining and analyzing the lists of citing sources, you must read every potentially relevant source in the cite list. If time allows, you should read every citing source to determine its impact on the case you are updating. Reading the citing sources in chronological order will give you a sense of how the law has developed as it was applied in various situations. If you are pressed for time, prioritize the citing sources you will read according to the following criteria:

- Read cases from your jurisdiction before reading cases decided elsewhere, which are only persuasive authority.

- Read cases from the highest appellate court, then the intermediate appellate courts, and finally the trial courts (if trial court cases are published) in that jurisdiction.

- Focus on any negative treatment. Look for any case that reverses, overrules, criticizes, or distinguishes your case.

- Choose cases cited for the headnotes that are on point for your research.

II. When to Update

Updating is a valuable research tool at several points in the research process. First, quickly check the colored symbol of a case you are reading online so that you will know immediately whether a case has been treated negatively. If so, you may want to explore that treatment before beginning to place much reliance on the case's analysis.

Later, when you have determined that a case is relevant to your research, carefully review its list of citing sources to find other cases and secondary sources that discuss the same points of law as the first case. Reading the citing sources produced by an updating search may lead to cases in which the court's reasoning is explained more fully or to cases with facts more similar to yours. As you discover more cases that are on point for your issue, look for trends in frequency and treatment of case citations. In general, cases that have been cited frequently and followed extensively should form the basis of your analysis. You may exclude a case that has been ignored by later cases unless its facts are very similar to yours or the reasoning is especially relevant. You will have to counter in your analysis any line of cases that criticize or distinguish your case.

You should continue updating the cases and other authorities you cite in a brief or memo until the day your final document is submitted. The case you updated two weeks ago could have been overruled yesterday. With online updating so widely available, courts expect the authorities cited in a brief to be current as of the date of filing. Supervising attorneys have similar expectations.

III. Updating Other Authorities

While this chapter has used a case as the primary example of updating, many additional authorities from both federal and state jurisdictions can be updated online, including statutes, constitutions, administrative regulations, attorney general opinions, law review articles, and restatements. Coverage varies among states and among online services.

Using KeyCite or Shepard's for statutes can provide information similar to annotated statutory codes, including history information and a list of cases that have cited a particular statutory provision. The treatment codes and colored symbols will mean slightly different things, because statutes are not "overruled" or "affirmed," but these meanings are explained on the Westlaw and Lexis websites. Updating regulations with KeyCite or Shepard's is typically more productive in federal research than in state research. If you are researching a Florida administrative rule, using the updating tools described in Chapter 4, Administrative Law, will be more helpful.

Finally, remember that KeyCiting or Shepardizing secondary sources will typically only reveal whether they have been cited, not how current they are. The fact that a secondary source has been cited is only one of a number of factors to consider when using the source, as explained in Chapter 6.

IV. Ethics

Your obligation of providing competent representation to a client, by definition, includes updating your research to be sure you are advising or advocating for your client based on the best available information. Moreover, courts expect lawyers to update their authorities. At both the trial and appellate level, courts rely on advocates not only to provide support for their arguments, but also to present the current state of the law. A failure to cite current law or disclose adverse authority may result in sanctions, malpractice suits, public embarrassment, and damage to your reputation.

In a recent case, Florida's Fifth District Court of Appeal "admonish[ed] counsel to be more thorough in their research. Had this [controlling] authority been identified earlier, this frivolous proceeding might have been avoided. Competent legal research is the responsibility of counsel."[6] The Second District Court of Appeal has noted that lawyers are "expected to use computer-assisted legal research to ensure that their research is complete and up-to-date."[7] In an earlier case, the Third District Court of Appeal criticized an attorney for relying on an outdated case when updating would have revealed the case had been questioned.[8]

---

6. *Bonilla v. State*, 62 So. 3d 1233, 1234 (5th DCA 2011).

7. *Hagopian v. Justice Admin. Comm'n*, 18 So. 3d 625, 642 (Fla. 2d DCA 2009) (noting the high costs of online services).

8. *See Glassalum Eng'g Corp. v. 392208 Ontario Ltd.*, 487 So. 2d 87, 88 (Fla. 3d DCA 1986) (noting that the court was forced to rely on its own research because counsel for both parties "performed inadequately"). In another instance, the judge ordered a major law firm to copy for each of its partners and associates an opinion chastising the firm for failing to cite a case adverse to the client's argument. The judge stated in the opinion, "For counsel to have been unaware of those cases means that they did not Shepardize their principal authority...." *Golden Eagle Distribg. Corp. v. Burroughs Corp.*, 103 F.R.D. 124, 129 (N.D. Cal. 1984).

Chapter 6

Secondary Sources

I. Introduction

In legal research, "secondary sources" are sources that discuss, describe, or comment on the law, without having the force of law themselves. Examples include law review articles, legal encyclopedias, and books or treatises.

Secondary sources can provide shortcuts to primary authority, and can give helpful background or context for understanding an issue or an area of the law. Always remember, however, that only primary authorities have the force of law. When analyzing a problem, predicting how a court will rule, or trying to convince a court to agree with your position, your goal will be to locate whatever primary authority is available.

This chapter begins with an overview of when to use secondary sources, how to choose among the variety available, and how to update them. The rest of this chapter is devoted to specific secondary sources, both in print and online.

A. When to Use Secondary Sources

Secondary sources are aids to both research and comprehension. You should always start with a secondary source when researching an unfamiliar area of law. Quickly reading a legal encyclopedia entry, for example, can help you understand the basic concepts of that area of law. Some secondary sources are written to assist practitioners in specific areas of the law and can provide a helpful overview of basic concepts. Even the most general secondary source will often reveal key words that will enable you to find pertinent cases; other sources will take you directly to cases.

As your research progresses, you will often find that reading or re-reading secondary sources helps you to clarify your own analysis of a problem. For example, you might find a law review article discussing the tort of "negligent infliction of emotional distress." Your first reading of the article will take you to cases discussing the law; after reading those cases, you might profit from re-reading the article to compare your own analysis of the law to the author's. This does not mean the source should be cited as authority. The text of a secondary source is never binding authority. Even an article written by a renowned expert is, at best, persuasive.

As attorneys become more expert in certain areas, they rely on secondary sources less for basic explanations or overviews, and more as sources of commentary, policy, and current developments in the law. Even experienced attorneys, however, are regularly confronted with problems they have not had to solve before and can benefit from what a wide range of secondary sources has to offer.

B. How to Choose Secondary Sources

Although the volume of materials available can be intimidating, lawyers learn with experience to eliminate some potential sources and select others. When beginning research in an area of law that is completely new to you, the most helpful sources will likely be those that are broad and general, such as treatises or legal encyclopedias. In some states, a legal encyclopedia specific to that state will often serve as a shortcut not only to understanding basic rules of law, but also to finding primary sources that illustrate the rules. For example, *Florida Jurisprudence (Second)* summarizes Florida law on a wide variety of substantive and procedural topics. Other legal encyclopedias can also be used as case-finding tools but, because their coverage is more general, they are not always as helpful in researching the law of a specific state.

Once you have narrowed the issue, or if you are researching an issue in an area where you already have a solid background, you might choose sources that analyze more narrow points of law, such as *American Law Reports* annotations or most law review articles. The descriptions of various sources provided below are intended, among other things, to help you determine which sources are helpful for certain types of issues.

When you have a good grasp of the area of law you are researching and are finding helpful primary authorities, do not feel you have to keep searching for every possible secondary source. Continue researching using primary sources, and come back to secondary sources to the extent they help you deepen or clarify your analysis.[1]

---

1. Photocopying or printing secondary sources is expensive, time-consuming, and wasteful. Keep good notes about the sources you have consulted, and photocopy or print only specific portions that you will refer to as you write. Note-taking is discussed in Chapter 1.

C. Updating Secondary Sources — In General

Many secondary sources cannot be Shepardized or KeyCited to determine whether they are still current or respected. As you use various sources, you will see that there are other methods for determining whether your source reflects the current state of the law. Many print sources include pocket parts or paper supplements, which should be checked diligently. Even though secondary sources cannot be "overruled," it is important to update your research.

II. Legal Periodicals

A. Overview

Legal periodicals publish articles on every aspect of the law, with emphasis ranging from the extremely theoretical to the solidly practical.

Many legal periodicals are published in the form of law reviews. Law review articles are often a good place to start learning about an unfamiliar area because they summarize the law, analyze new developments in the law, and provide background information on important cases and new statutes. Law reviews are generally published by students at law schools, although some are exclusively written and edited by experts in a given field. Each law school has a law review or journal that publishes articles on a variety of topics. Most law schools also have more specialized journals devoted to such areas as environmental law, civil rights, or tax. Law schools within a particular state often devote specific issues to recent legislation or case law developments from that jurisdiction.

Law reviews contain several different types of articles. Those specifically labeled "Articles" are generally written by practitioners or scholars, not students, and provide in-depth analysis of a specific, sometimes quite narrow point of law. Occasionally, they will contain a survey of a particular area instead of analysis of a narrow topic. Other pieces, usually labeled "Comments," may be less comprehensive. A typical student-written piece is a "Case Comment," which analyzes a single case in depth. Students also write "Notes," which may be as long and detailed as articles. Law reviews also sometime designate shorter pieces as "Essays" or some similar designation.

Legal periodicals also encompass bar journals, bar newspapers, and journals specific to a certain topic area or type of practice. Examples include *The Florida Bar Journal*, *The Florida Bar News*, and the *Trial Advocate Quarterly*, published by the Florida Defense Lawyers Association. Articles in these publications tend to be more practical and less "scholarly," but can still be helpful in your research. Because they tend to have shorter publication schedules than scholarly journals, they can be good sources of information on recent developments or in areas of the law that are evolving in your jurisdiction.

When selecting an article to read, relying on an article in formulating or deepening your analysis, or deciding whether to cite an article in your written work, you must take into account the persuasive value of the article. There are no hard-and-fast rules for preferring one source to another. In general, you will prefer an article written by an expert or experienced practitioner in a field to one written by a student or recent graduate. However, there is no reason to totally disregard student pieces. Given the amount of research necessary to prepare a piece for publication, a law student may know more about a particular topic than many practitioners. Student pieces can be particularly helpful in summarizing or surveying the developments in a field. Regardless of authorship, the footnotes in most articles have been gathered and verified by student editors. Table 6-1 summarizes key factors to weigh in choosing articles.

Table 6-1. Factors to Weigh in Choosing Articles

1. Has the article already been widely cited as authoritative by courts or other writers?

2. How recent is the article? In an area of the law that is relatively stable, or when you are researching the evolution of a law or doctrine, you may find useful information in an older article; in more rapidly changing areas, you will usually want to start with the most recent articles you can find.

3. Is the author already recognized as an authority in the field? If the biographical information about the author reveals that the author is a practitioner, scholar, or judge, it is relatively easy to find out what some of the author's other publications are and to get an idea of how frequently the author has published in the past.

4. Is the journal published in the jurisdiction you are researching?

5. Is the article solidly supported with reference to both primary and secondary authorities?

B. Locating Periodicals

There are two major periodical indexes: the *Index to Legal Periodicals and Books* (ILPB) and the *Current Law Index* (CLI). These indexes exist in print, but are most commonly used in electronic versions. The *Index to Legal Periodicals and Books* is available on Westlaw. The electronic companion to the CLI is available on Westlaw as the *Legal Resource Index*. Most law libraries have links to them that you can access from your computer. Most law libraries also have links to the *Current Index to Legal Periodicals* (CILP), which is published weekly and is also available on Westlaw, and the *Index to Foreign Legal Periodicals*, which is helpful in researching issues of international law.

ILPB began indexing "scholarly" publications, primarily law reviews, in 1908; CLI began indexing a broader range of publications, including bar journals and legal newspapers, in 1980. Thus, you should choose ILPB if you are looking for a specific article or topic published prior to 1980. (You may have to consult paper versions of the indexes for older articles, as well; ask a reference librarian for help if this is the case.) For more recent years, CLI may provide a broader result. If all you are looking for is an article to get you started in an area, you can use either index; if you are doing a more exhaustive search (for example, in preparation for writing an article of your own) you should check both.

The most common way of using online indexes is through key word searching that allows you to retrieve articles on a given topic, such as "at-will employment." You can find articles by searching for subjects or specific authors.

When using the online indexes, remember that you are searching just the titles and abstracts of the articles listed there, not the full text of the articles. If you search for "employment" and the title of an article refers to "employees' rights," you will not retrieve that article. Moreover, a source is not necessarily on point just because a key word appears in the title or abstract. These indexes make no judgments about the quality or content of an article; all they tell you is that your search term appears in the title or abstract of an article. You may miss helpful articles if you frame your request too narrowly.

Because of this limitation, some researchers use Westlaw and Lexis to search the full-text article databases instead of going through the indexes. At the beginning of your research, however, unless you are starting with a fairly discrete issue, full-text searching can be time-consuming and inefficient; your search terms may appear in a number of articles that are not relevant to your issue. Also, you need to be aware that the coverage of law reviews in Westlaw and

Lexis is not uniform; some journals are not carried on both services, and all issues are not available for all journals.[2]

An online archive of scholarly journals called JSTOR (for Journal Storage) is becoming increasingly useful in legal research. JSTOR collects not only legal journals, but also journals in a wide range of academic disciplines, and makes them available for full-text searching. JSTOR does not contain the full text of very recent articles, and its coverage varies depending on its agreement with specific publishers. If your research requires consulting extra-legal commentary sources or law review articles that may not be available through Lexis or Westlaw, JSTOR can be an extremely valuable tool. Most university libraries subscribe to JSTOR. Information about the archive is available at www.jstor.org.

Many law libraries also subscribe to an online service called HeinOnline, which publishes (in electronic form) journals in PDF format, so that what you see on the screen is what you would have read in the original journal. Like JSTOR, HeinOnline does not have the text of the most recent journals (which are often available on the website of the journal or law school in question), but it makes up for that with an archive that, in many cases, goes back to the original volume of the publication. For example, the HeinOnline archive includes copies of *Florida Law Review* from 1948; *Florida State University Law Review* from 1973; and *Stetson Law Review* from 1970. In addition to legal periodicals, HeinOnline provides online access to United States treaties and international agreements, Supreme Court opinions, Attorney General opinions, federal legislative histories, and much more. Information about its current holdings is available at http://heinonline.org.

C. The Role of Periodical Articles in Research

Law review articles are often a good place to begin legal research because they are extensively footnoted with citations to primary authority. Footnotes to primary authority are helpful whether the author of an article is a student or a scholar. Also, law review articles often give surveys or overviews of the law that will be helpful to introduce you to a topic. (Some articles, however,

---

2. Both Westlaw and Lexis provide information on the contents of various databases. On WestlawNext, click on the small "i" on the search screen to see the current scope of each database. On Lexis Advance, go to "Browse Sources," locate the source in the index, click on the name of the source, and select "View all information for this source." For general research, it often will not matter whether you search law reviews in one service or the other, but if you are trying to locate a specific article you may find that it is only available in one.

may be so specialized that only an attorney with a general knowledge of the subject area will be able to put the article in context.)

Law review articles also can be helpful in analyzing changing or controversial areas because many authors write articles to critique existing or proposed laws. Remember that a single author's position does not necessarily reflect the state of the law or of scholarly opinion. Do your own analysis of the pertinent cases, statutes, and other primary authority.

Do not feel you must read a given number of articles before proceeding to the next step in your research. Keep the goal of your research in mind. Most of the time, that goal will be understanding the area of law at issue and locating primary authority.

D. Updating and Citing Law Review Articles

Unlike most other legal research materials, law review articles and other periodicals are never "updated." That is, once an article is published it is not revised and brought up-to-date with subsequent developments in the law. You cannot be sure an article still correctly describes the state of the law without doing further research. You can find out whether courts or other writers have cited a scholarly article, however, by using Shepard's or KeyCite. Alternatively, you can search a case law database by author or title to see whether courts have cited a particular article.[3]

As a general rule, do not cite directly to an article in an office memo or a court document when you could support the same proposition with primary authority. Even if you are analyzing a case that is discussed in an article, read the case and cite directly to it. Cite the article only if you are referring to the author's unique analysis or insight.

Articles may be cited in some limited situations, such as when they summarize original research that would not be available anywhere else. Articles can also be cited when they allow you to (1) avoid citing a lengthy list of authorities to expand on a point you have already supported with primary authority; (2) provide background information to the reader; (3) summarize the law of several jurisdictions; or (4) discuss the history of a law or doctrine. Note that even in these situations, you can often find what you need in a case: especially at the highest level, or when treating an issue of first impression, courts will often preface their analysis with an overview of the law.

---

3. Studies indicate that law review articles are rarely cited in court decisions; most are never cited, but this does not mean they cannot be valuable research tools.

The two major citation manuals, the *ALWD Guide* and the *Bluebook,* both contain rules governing all aspects of citing articles, from the author's name to the abbreviation for each journal published.[4] Both manuals contain standard abbreviations for periodical names and require you to indicate whether an article is student-written when citing the article in a brief or memo.

You will often, but not always, need to use signals and parentheticals when citing secondary sources. A frequently used signal is *see generally,* which indicates that the source provides helpful background information about your topic.

III. Treatises

A. Overview

The term "treatise" is used to describe a variety of books on legal subjects. Almost any legal text could be called a treatise. Treatises are invaluable as introductions to a subject area and can be helpful to a lesser extent in locating cases. Treatises include exhaustive surveys of the law of a given area, along with case citations; scholarly discussions of an area; analyses of new legal developments; and black-letter or "law in a nutshell" publications. Figure 6-1 contains an excerpt from a widely respected treatise on Florida evidence law.

B. Locating Treatises

The most direct route to finding treatises on a given subject is to search a library's online catalog by key word or title. Once you have found pertinent titles and the call numbers assigned to them, the old-fashioned trick of "browsing the stacks" is still often helpful, as well. By browsing the stacks in the area where those call numbers are shelved, you will often discover treatises that title searching, alone, did not reveal.

Another way to find a title is to check the casebooks, hornbooks, and other treatises you already have.[5] Many books contain a list of legal texts from the

---

4. See Chapter 9 for additional information about legal citation.

5. Note that a casebook is not a treatise; it collects fragments of cases and other authorities with only limited commentary or explanation of the authorities. Casebooks are rarely referred to outside of the law school classroom. Hornbooks are, in contrast, very basic treatises. You may find them useful to refresh your memory about basic legal concepts, particularly in "bread and butter" subjects like torts, contracts, and civil procedure, but they are less useful as a springboard to primary authorities than many other treatises and secondary sources.

Figure 6-1. Excerpt from *Florida Evidence*

Source: WestlawNext. Reprinted with permission of Thomson Reuters.

same publisher. Using any one of those titles, you can obtain a call number and browse the stacks.

An online service, www.Indexmaster.com, allows users to search the indexes and tables of contents of thousands of legal books. If you have access to this subscription service, which is provided by some libraries, you can use it to locate treatises addressing specific topics or issues of interest. This is particularly helpful if you are looking for a treatise that provides in-depth coverage of a limited area rather than a general overview of the law. Once you have identified a potentially helpful treatise, you can determine whether your library already has a copy or request assistance in obtaining one.

The number of legal treatises available online in full-text format is still small in comparison to periodical articles and other sources, but growing. Both Lexis and Westlaw make available a number of treatises published by affiliated companies. Click through "Browse" for "Secondary Sources" then "Texts and Treatises" on WestlawNext, or use the "Browse Sources" feature on Lexis Advance to explore what sources are available in each service.

C. The Role of Treatises in Research

Like periodicals, treatises are often an excellent place to begin research, especially in an unfamiliar area. They can also be helpful starting points when you are researching areas of the law that are well established. By starting with a treatise instead of searching directly for cases or statutes, you can save considerable time and frustration. Even if the treatise does not cite a relevant case or statute in your jurisdiction, it will help you develop a list of key words to use in searching those primary authorities.

Some treatises attempt to summarize a body of law in a single volume. These are most helpful for learning basic rules of law and avoiding outdated or discredited ones. Other treatises are multi-volume works containing extensive case citations to a number of jurisdictions. A third type of treatise concentrates on explaining specific aspects of state law. For example, if you were about to handle an appeal in Florida and had specific questions about appellate practice within the state, you could consult *Florida Appellate Practice*, a treatise by Judge Philip Padovano of the First District Court of Appeal. A treatise may be helpful even if your problem is specific; treatises exist on an endless variety of topics.

If you need information about the law of several or all states, look for treatises devoted to surveys of the law. Sources such as the *Nutshell* series (published by West) and hornbooks can be helpful starting points for understanding an unfamiliar area. They generally have only limited case citations, but make up for that with concise explanations of the basic concepts you will be analyzing.

In almost all of these situations the role of the treatise is to inform, to expand your understanding of the subject area, and to point you towards primary authorities.

D. Updating and Citing Treatises

Some single-volume books are not updated except by the publication of subsequent editions. Consequently, even an authoritative work may be less helpful in research than a more recent publication by a different author.

Many treatises are updated, however, meaning that they are revised or supplemented to reflect changes in the law. Multi-volume treatises are often published in looseleaf binders that allow discussions of new cases to be added without reprinting the entire volume. Sometimes discussions of new cases are simply inserted at the beginning of the volume with cross references to the sections in the main part of the volume. Other treatises are supplemented using pocket parts or paperback supplements. Always check the publication date of your treatise, and always check to see if it is updated using one of these methods. When using a treatise online, be sure to check how recently it has been updated.

Avoid citing treatises in office memos or court documents unless they are among the small number regarded as authoritative. For example, *Moore's Federal Practice* is widely regarded as authoritative on federal procedural issues and is sometimes cited in court decisions. Within Florida, *Florida Appellate Practice* is well respected on appellate practice issues; *Florida Evidence*, by Charles W. Ehrhardt, is regarded as highly authoritative on issues arising out of the Evidence Code. An easy way to see whether Florida courts have relied on a particular treatise is to search for the author's name or for the title in a database for Florida cases on either Westlaw or Lexis.

Citing a treatise for a helpful summary or comparison of the laws of several states may be appropriate. As with periodicals, you may cite treatises as additional authority to expand on a point you have already supported through primary sources. When citing a treatise as additional authority, you would typically introduce the cite with a signal and add a parenthetical explaining why the treatise is helpful. These signals and accompanying parenthetical phrases tell the reader that, in addition to the primary authority supporting your proposition, background material clarifies or expands your discussion. If you are not sure whether you can cite a treatise as authoritative, err on the side of using primary authority. You should not cite treatises in place of your own analysis.

ALWD and the *Bluebook* govern the citation of books, pamphlets, and nonperiodic materials. The citation format is different from what you may be accustomed to in other academic writing. The cite typically includes the author's name, full book title, page number, and date.

IV. CLE Materials

A. Overview

Continuing Legal Education (CLE) is mandatory in most jurisdictions, including Florida. CLE instructors are typically practitioners in a particular specialty, judges, or, sometimes, law professors. Many CLE programs include written materials. Some CLE materials consist of whatever the instructor or course sponsor has developed as a course handout. They are not extensive, but can be helpful research tools because of their practical emphasis. Other CLE publications are very similar to treatises and are written to provide a comprehensive discussion of practice in a certain area. Examples include *Florida Administrative Practice*; *Florida Juvenile Law and Practice*; and *Florida Eminent Domain Practice and Procedure*, all published by the CLE Publications of The Florida Bar.

B. Locating CLE Materials

CLE materials are catalogued like other library materials and shelved according to subject (by call number). You can search for CLE materials directly in the same way that you would search for treatises (in fact, a search of an online catalog will typically retrieve both types of sources). For materials specific to Florida, you also can go to the Lexis bookstore for Florida materials, www.lexisnexis.com/flabar/. Once you have a specific title in mind, you can retrieve it from a library's catalog.

Two of the largest CLE publishers are the Practising Law Institute (PLI) and the American Law Institute-American Bar Association (ALI-ABA). Some of their materials are available online; you can use their names as key words in an index search. The PLI home page is at www.pli.edu. The ALI-ABA home page is at www.ali-aba.org. Both allow searching for CLE titles.

A number of CLE publications and practice tools are available on both Westlaw and Lexis. The advantage of these versions, as with periodicals and other sources, is full-text searching to retrieve helpful titles. This is not necessarily more effective than simply going through an index, though, because titles of CLE publications are often specific enough to indicate whether materials will be helpful. The major disadvantage is coverage; the services do not have the same coverage, and neither can be considered comprehensive, although titles are added constantly.

Some of the major CLE providers also have websites where you can search for a title that seems relevant to your research issue. Because these are commercial sites, however, you will not be able to retrieve the full text of the CLE publications; you will find only titles, sometimes abstracts, and ordering information. Still, this can be a useful way of locating potentially helpful titles, and you can then check your library catalog to see which titles are available to you in hard copy.

C. Beginning Research with CLE Materials

CLE materials are excellent resources for learning about a developing area of the law. Because the materials are written for practitioners, they are often specific to a particular jurisdiction. Often a significant statute or case in one jurisdiction will be the subject of a CLE course within a few months of the enactment or decision. If your research involves interpreting a recent statute or case, an area that is subject to changing regulations such as environmental law, or a rapidly evolving area such as intellectual property, you should always check for CLE materials on point.

CLE materials can also be very helpful when you are just learning about an area, for the same reasons that attending a course in that area would be helpful.

D. Updating and Citing CLE Materials

CLE materials are not updated, although sometimes they may be published in revised versions; you should look for the most recent publication date under a given topic. You must do further research to determine whether a particular volume is still current. One method would be to Shepardize or KeyCite the cases or statutes discussed in the CLE materials themselves.

CLE materials are not considered "scholarly" and thus are not cited in legal writing. Rarely you may see a CLE publication (such as an ALI-ABA handbook) cited in a judicial opinion; as a rule, however, you should use them only as starting points for your own research.

V. Legal Encyclopedias

A. Overview

Legal encyclopedias cover an extensive range of topics. They provide an overview of a legal area, and in established areas such as torts and contracts are often as helpful as a treatise or hornbook. The text in encyclopedias is general, but is typically supported by extensive footnotes to cases from state and federal jurisdictions that illustrate the point of law being discussed. These extensive footnotes and the editorial process of well-established publishers ensure that information in a legal encyclopedia is reliable.

In Florida, state law is summarized in *Florida Jurisprudence (Second)*, a state encyclopedia known as "Fla. Jur." An excerpt from this encyclopedia is provided in Figure 6-2. Two national law encyclopedias contain entries on the law of all American jurisdictions, arranged alphabetically by topic. They are *Corpus Juris*

Secundum (CJS) and *American Jurisprudence (Second)* (Am. Jur.).[6] An excerpt from Am. Jur. appears later in this chapter in Figure 6-3. Because of the wide scope of their coverage, the national encyclopedias will not always lead you to cases from the jurisdiction you are working in. They do not focus on the law of specific jurisdictions, but usually indicate when there is a split of authority on a point of law. In addition to these general sources, some encyclopedias focus on a single area of the law.

B. Using Encyclopedias

When an issue is specific to Florida, Fla. Jur. will often be preferable to either of the national encyclopedias. Choosing between the two national encyclopedias is largely a matter of personal preference. Some people find one more helpful than another; others like the quantity of footnotes in one or the cross references in another.

1. *Florida Jurisprudence (Second)*

When your research project depends entirely on Florida law, you may choose to start your research in *Florida Jurisprudence (Second)*. The encyclopedia is organized into major topics, and contains both topic and index volumes. In addition to the general index, you can use a volume titled "Words and Phrases" to find a specific section. For example, the phrase "malpractice insurance" gives a reference to the Florida statutory definition of malpractice insurance as well as to a Fla. Jur. section discussing it.

Each topic is preceded by both a general and a specific table of contents for that topic. Fla. Jur. also begins each topic with "Scope" and "Treated Elsewhere" paragraphs; always skim these before reading the main text. The Treated Elsewhere paragraph indicates whether specific aspects of your topic, or closely related topics, are discussed in a separate section of the encyclopedia.

If you already have a citation to primary authority, you can find a relevant encyclopedia section by using one of several helpful tables in Fla. Jur. These include the "Table of Cases," which are separate volumes that allow you to find sections using a case citation, and a "Table of Laws and Rules" volume that will refer you to sections discussing particular statutes. The tables also refer to a wide variety of state and federal practice tools and other reference

---

6. Some legal research texts discuss cross-referencing between older and newer versions of both encyclopedias. In the rare instance that you might need to work with an older version, speak with a reference librarian.

Figure 6-2. Excerpt from *Florida Jurisprudence (Second)*

§ 172 FLORIDA JURISPRUDENCE 2D

removed in time as to deprive the circumstances of any evidentiary value and where nothing was presented by the customer to suggest that conditions in the health inspector's report caused the customer's illness or that these conditions even existed on the day in question.[11]

A court may determine that similar evidence is not admissible as too remote under one set of facts and is admissible as not too remote under another.[12]

2. Unfair Prejudice

§ 173 Generally

Research References

West's Key Number Digest, Evidence ⚷99 to 117
Am. Jur. Pleading and Practice Forms, Evidence § 20 (Notice of Motion—to exclude prejudicial evidence)

Even after determining that evidence is relevant, a trial court in every case must also consider the evidence rule requiring weighing of relevancy against unfair prejudice.[1] The trial court should be given wide discretion in determining whether the probative value of evidence is outweighed substantially by the likelihood of undue prejudice.[2] Even if evidence is relevant, a trial court is required statutorily to balance the danger of unfair prejudice against the probative value of the evidence sought to be introduced, and the ap-

---

[11] Gallagher v. L.K. Restaurant & Motels, Inc., 481 So. 2d 562 (Fla. Dist. Ct. App. 5th Dist. 1986).

[12] Thompson v. U.S. Sugar Corp., 548 So. 2d 1171 (Fla. Dist. Ct. App. 4th Dist. 1989) (no abuse of discretion in excluding testimony of driver's witnesses that three weeks after accident, warning lights at crossing were not working on the ground that the evidence was so remote as to be without probative value); Jones v. Stamper, 336 So. 2d 1251 (Fla. Dist. Ct. App. 1st Dist. 1976) (testimony of expert witness in automobile reconstruction that headlights of one vehicle were not on at time of collision was admissible where expert examined photographs taken at time of accident and where there was no evidence that vehicle had been tampered with in wrecking yard even though expert's examination of vehicle occurred 10 months after accident).

[Section 173]

[1] Floyd v. State, 913 So. 2d 564 (Fla. 2005).

[2] Stephens v. State, 787 So. 2d 747 (Fla. 2001); Pulcini v. State, 41 So. 3d 338 (Fla. Dist. Ct. App. 4th Dist. 2010); Wilchcombe v. State, 842 So. 2d 198 (Fla. Dist. Ct. App. 3d Dist. 2003).

236

Source: *Florida Jurisprudence (Second)*. Reprinted with permission of Thomson Reuters.

books. For example, separate volumes of Fla. Jur. called "Pleadings and Practice Forms," list the elements of proof for specific causes of action under Florida law.

Fla. Jur. is updated with pocket parts. Online it is available on both Lexis and Westlaw, but the Westlaw version may be more current because West currently publishes the encyclopedia.

2. Corpus Juris Secundum

The original goal of the CJS publishers was to include every reported case in American law. In recent years, they have stopped including all cases.

CJS has a number of finding tools that allow you to locate information within the encyclopedia. CJS is arranged into broad topics, which it calls "titles," such as "Torts." Each title is further divided into numbered sections. Each "topic volume" of CJS contains a list of the titles discussed in the encyclopedia. You can use this list to determine which titles may be relevant. Next, at the beginning of each title there are two outlines of the subjects discussed under that general heading, arranged by section number. One outline is general and will help you pinpoint a portion of the title for further exploration; the second outline is more detailed and will refer you to a specific section number.

CJS also has separate "General Index" volumes that you can use to search for relevant topics using key words. The index will refer you to a title and section number that correspond to your key word. In general, however, if you know the broad area of the law that applies to your research problem, you will often be able to use the title outlines in the topic volumes to go directly to the sections you need. If you have not found material on point using one approach, try the other.

Other publications often have references directly to a CJS title and section. CJS uses the West key number system, which allows you to locate cases on a pertinent topic regardless of jurisdiction. The key number system is discussed more fully in Chapter 2.

CJS relies on pocket parts to supplement bound topic volumes. Always check the pocket part of the volume you are working with. The supplement may contain new text in addition to more footnotes. In older volumes, the key numbers may appear only in the pocket parts. From time to time an entire volume will be reprinted, and that volume, in turn, will have its own pocket part for more recent cases. The CJS index is annually updated in paperback pamphlets.

CJS is available on Westlaw. Its full text can be searched through terms and connectors or natural language searching. An alternate approach is to review the table of contents, which Westlaw also provides.

3. *American Jurisprudence (Second)*

The original goal of *American Jurisprudence* (Am. Jur.) was less comprehensive, more selective coverage of American law than that provided by CJS. In addition to case references, Am. Jur. footnotes also contain citations to annotations in *American Law Reports*, discussed later in this chapter.[7]

Like CJS, Am. Jur. has a list of topics, at the front of the supplement to volume 1, and a general index. It is often easier to begin research with the index volumes.

In the Am. Jur. index volumes, in addition to the general index, you will find a "Table of Abbreviations," which is actually a list of the general topics

Figure 6-3. Excerpt from *American Jurisprudence (Second)*

⬅ Previous   Next ➡
2 Am Jur 2d Adoption § 5 (Copy citation)

American Jurisprudence, Second Edition > **Adoption** > **I. In General** > **B. Origin and Legal Basis of Adoption; Adoption Statutes**

Author

Tracy Farrell, J.D., Rosemary Gregor, J.D., Anne Payne, J.D., Lisa Zakowlski, J.D.

§ 5 Origin and legal basis

There is no fundamental right to adopt.[n1] Nor does the interest in adopting a child fall within the marital privacy right, since the adoption statutes require adopters to submit their personal lives to intensive scrutiny before the adoption may be approved.[n2]

Adoption has been practiced since ancient times.[n3] Even so, adoption is not a natural right[n4] and is unknown at common law.[n5] Rather, it is of wholly statutory origin[n6] and is in derogation of the common law.[n7] Any attempt to grant rights to the natural relatives, in the absence of statutory authority, is against public policy and is void.[n8]

One cannot be the legally adopted child of another by private agreement unless there is statutory authority for doing so,[n9] although a court of equity may, where justice requires, decree a person to have rights of an adopted child -- that is to have been "equitably adopted" -- for purposes of inheritance, under certain circumstances.[n10]

Source: WestlawNext. Reprinted with permission of Thomson Reuters.

---

7. The footnotes also contain references to practice tools such as *American Jurisprudence Trials* and *American Jurisprudence Proof of Facts*, which are discussed in Chapter 7.

covered in the encyclopedia. You can use these to target a section of the general index that will contain references to your topic.

In Am. Jur., each topic is preceded by a table of contents. Am. Jur. has an additional helpful feature at the beginning of each general topic, the "Treated Elsewhere" paragraph. Once you have identified a relevant topic, you should always skim through the Treated Elsewhere paragraph before reading the rest of the section.

If you are researching a question of federal law, Am. Jur. has a "Table of Laws and Rules" that will take you directly to each section of the encyclopedia that discusses any federal statutes, rules, or regulations.

Like CJS, Am. Jur. uses pocket parts to supplement bound volumes. Occasionally, when the pocket parts become too bulky, the publishers will publish a separate paper supplement to a topic volume. In principle, these are shelved next to the bound volumes they supplement; if your volume does not have a pocket part, take the time to look for the supplement.

Am. Jur. also has a "New Topic Service" contained in a separate binder that is shelved with the Am. Jur. index volumes. While pocket parts supplement topics that already appear in the bound volumes, the New Topic Service contains entirely new topics, along with citations to cases and annotations.

Am. Jur. is available on both Lexis and Westlaw. Like CJS, it can be searched with terms and connectors, in natural language, and through a table of contents function.

C. The Role of Encyclopedias in Research

Like some basic treatises, encyclopedias provide a broad overview of the law. They are most useful early in your research. A state law encyclopedia may be more helpful on issues within a particular jurisdiction than national encyclopedias, but even a state law encyclopedia is only a starting point for your research.

D. Updating and Citing Encyclopedias

As noted above, print encyclopedias are typically supplemented with a combination of pocket parts and other tools. Online databases should not be assumed to be more current than their print counterparts. Always check the series you are using to see how it is updated. Keep in mind that there can be a long lead time between developments in the law and their addition to an encyclopedia; encyclopedias are rarely a good source of recent developments.

According to *ALWD* and the *Bluebook*, legal encyclopedias are cited by volume, topic and section number. As a rule, however, you should avoid citing to encyclopedias in office memos or court documents.[8]

VI. *American Law Reports*

A. Overview

ALR refers to *American Law Reports*, a hybrid case reporter and commentary source. The original goal of ALR was to serve as a highly selective case reporter; over time it has come to be used primarily for its detailed "annotations," or commentaries on specific topics that accompany the reported cases. Annotation topics are often similar to periodical articles in scope and length; they address specific topics in detail rather than providing broad overviews of the law. The first page of an annotation is shown in Figure 6-4.

For example, a legal encyclopedia might have a general overview of a landowner's duties to those who enter her land. An annotation, on the other hand, might address the landowner's duty to a specific category of persons (social guests, rescue personnel, undiscovered trespassers) and would identify conflicts in the law or splits in authority on that particular point.[9]

ALR has been published in several series. The series you are most likely to use are the most recently published: ALR3d, ALR4th, ALR5th, ALR6th, and two sets of federal law annotations, ALR Fed. and ALR Fed. 2d. The non-federal series deal almost exclusively with state law topics (volumes of ALR3d published between 1965 and 1969 contain federal law topics as well); the two federal series deal specifically with federal law from 1969 to the present.

B. Locating Annotations

Unlike a legal encyclopedia, ALR is not organized according to topic. You cannot expect to find an annotation addressing your topic simply by finding

---

8. One federal appellate judge has stated that legal encyclopedias "[s]hould be cited only in the following manner: 'See cases collected at.... '" Ruggero J. Aldisert, *Winning on Appeal: Better Briefs and Oral Argument* 105 (2d ed. 2003).

9. As an example, the following titles come from 21 ALR6th: "Substantive Challenges to Propriety of Execution by Lethal Injection in State Capital Proceedings"; "Common-Law Liability for Injury Caused by Fireworks or Firecracker"; "Construction and Application of 'Tail' Insurance Policies"; and "Liability of Employer, Supervisor, or Manager for Intentionally Causing Employee Emotional Distress—Accusation or Implication of Employee's Dishonesty."

Figure 6-4. Excerpt from *American Law Reports*

WestlawNext™   Q▾ Search American Law Reports - Products Liability   SEARCH   advan

Liability of Food Manufacturer Based on Statement in Product Labeling or Promotion Relating to, or Inconsistent with
American Law Reports ALR6th   Originally published in 2014   *(Approx. 30 pages)*

| Document | History (0) | Citing References (18) ▾ | Table of Authorities | *Powered by* KeyCite |

◀ Return to list   ◀ **6 of 10 results** ▶   ◀▾   Q▾

92 A.L.R.6th 141 (Originally published in 2014)

American Law Reports
ALR6th
The ALR databases are made current by the weekly addition of relevant new cases.

Liability of Food Manufacturer Based on Statement in Product Labeling or
Promotion Relating to, or Inconsistent with Presence of, Trans Fat in Product

Robin Miller, J.D.

Consuming trans fat increases low-density lipoprotein ("bad") cholesterol, and current dietary
guidelines recommend that individuals keep trans fat consumption as low as possible. Consumers
have filed actions against food manufacturers in a variety of circumstances asserting that
statements by the manufacturer relating to trans fat in the manufacturer's products were untrue or
misleading. For example, in Askin v. Quaker Oats Co., 818 F. Supp. 2d 1081, 92 A.L.R.6th 679
(N.D. Ill. 2011), the court held that a consumer alleged an injury-in-fact sufficient to establish
standing to assert claims under Illinois law where the consumer alleged that the manufacturer lured
consumers into buying its oatmeal and granola products by touting the products as containing "0
grams trans fat" and being "wholesome" and "heart healthy" when in reality the products contained
unhealthy trans fats. This annotation collects and analyzes all the federal and state cases
discussing the liability, when not precluded by federal preemption, of a food manufacturer based

Source: WestlawNext. Reprinted with permission of Thomson Reuters.

a related topic in the main volume and browsing nearby sections. Thus, developing a good research vocabulary is essential to finding an ALR annotation on point.

All ALR series are currently indexed and digested together. Use the ALR indexes just as you use other indexes: search for key terms, which will lead you to entries describing annotations discussing those terms. If you are researching a specific statute, rule, or regulation, you can start with the separate "Table of Laws, Rules and Regulations" in the back of the index. The table will lead you directly to annotations citing your primary source. Similarly, if you are starting with a reference to a state court decision, separate volumes containing a "Table of Cases" may lead you to an annotation citing that decision. The Table of Cases is a relatively new feature, however, and only covers ALR5th and ALR6th. The ALR Digest is another method of finding annotations. It uses the West key number system.

Each annotation begins with a description of the scope of the annotation and a table of contents. You should always skim these sections before reading the entire annotation; you may find that another annotation addresses your issue more directly.

ALR is available for full-text searching on Westlaw and Lexis.

C. The Role of ALR Annotations in Research

Because ALR annotations are specific reports on limited legal issues, rather than general overviews of an area of law, you may want to turn to ALR only when you are familiar with the general area of law you are researching. If you know enough about your topic to frame it somewhat narrowly, an annotation may be a good starting point.

After determining that an annotation is on point, you can use it to find citations to primary authority on your issue. You can also use it to find extensive cross references to other annotations, encyclopedia entries, practice tools, and case digests (using West key numbers). In addition to the sources listed in the annotation, the case accompanying the annotation can lead to more cases through use of updating tools or digests.

Another benefit of ALR is the set of tables that accompany each annotation. Especially helpful early in your research will be a table that lists relevant cases by jurisdiction. Thus, even in an annotation with a national scope, you may find a list of cases specific to Florida.

Alternatively, you can begin your research with a different secondary source, and use the list of references in the annotation to double-check your own initial research.

D. Updating and Citing ALR Annotations

ALR uses pocket parts to supplement bound volumes, including index and digest volumes. An entire annotation will sometimes be superseded by a new annotation to reflect changes in the law. Always check to see whether an annotation is still current before you read and rely on it. The pocket parts of annotation volumes indicate whether an entire annotation has been superseded, as opposed to supplemented. Also, each ALR Index volume contains a comprehensive "Annotation History Table." If you locate an annotation by full-text searching on Westlaw, you will also see hyperlinks to the annotation's history. You can KeyCite annotations to find whether they have been cited in other legal sources. Annotations can also be Shepardized.

Despite their usefulness in research, annotations are infrequently cited in memos and court documents. In very limited circumstances, such as when a cite to an annotation will allow you to refer a reader to a lengthy list of cases illustrating a point, a citation to an annotation may be appropriate. Cite annotations by author, title, volume and page, and date. The author's name may not be available for older annotations; in that instance, use the designation "Annotation" before the annotation title. The *Bluebook* requires the designation "Annotation" before the annotation title, as well.

VII. Restatements

A. Overview

Restatements are scholarly treatments of areas of the law that attempt to set forth "black letter" rules of common law. They are among the most persuasive, and most often cited, of secondary sources.[10] If your research issue is governed exclusively by statutory or administrative law, however, the Restatements will not help you find primary authority on point.

If your issue is governed by common law in one of the Restatement areas, you can use the Restatement to find a statement of the common law rule, illustrations of the application of the rule, and cases in your jurisdiction that have cited the Restatement. Some of the Restatement areas are agency, conflict of laws, contracts, foreign relations, judgments, property, restitution, security, torts, law governing lawyers, and trusts.

The Restatements are published by the American Law Institute after extensive study and revision, and are edited by noted scholars, called "Reporters." The original goal of the Restatements was to produce a coherent statement of the common law that would have the weight of primary authority. Later, this goal was changed to allow drafters to predict the law based on emerging trends, not just to summarize existing law. Therefore, you cannot rely on the Restatements to provide a statement of the law in your jurisdiction. Your jurisdiction may be more progressive than the Restatement. Or your jurisdiction may have adopted one Restatement rule but not another, closely related rule. Always do further research into the law of your jurisdiction.

---

10. *See, e.g.*, Steven M. Barkan, Roy M. Mersky & Donald J. Dunn, *Fundamentals of Legal Research* 380 n.18 (9th ed. 2009) (according to ALI figures, Restatements had been cited 176,076 times by courts as of May 1, 2008).

B. Locating Applicable Restatement Sections and Cases Citing Them

Sometimes another source or case will cite directly to a Restatement section on point. If you do not have a cite, you must decide first which subject governs your issue and then which series you should use.

To date, Restatements have been published in three series, which do not all cover the same areas. For example, one of the subjects in the Third Series, the *Restatement (Third) of the Law of Unfair Competition*, was not treated as a separate topic in any of the earlier series.

In general, you will probably rely on the most recent series that addresses your topic. The original Restatements were published 50 or more years ago, and even in areas such as contracts and torts are less likely to help you understand the current state of the law than later series. However, you should not rule the earlier series out altogether.

Each series includes topic volumes, and some include index or appendix volumes, as explained below. The volumes often have a similar appearance. Therefore, you need to pay close attention to which volume you are using, as well as which series you are using.[11]

Finding a specific Restatement section requires a different approach depending on the series you are using. A "General Index" covers the subjects in the First Restatement, but not subsequent series. The Second and Third Series have no comprehensive index. Instead, you must look in one of two places: the front of each topic volume generally has a table of contents, and the final topic volume in each subject generally has an index of that subject. Remember to check both places.

Once you have located a pertinent Restatement rule, read the comments and illustrations that follow each "black letter" rule. The comments may tell you, among other things, the intended scope of the rule; whether the rule reflects a consensus view or a modern trend; and whether there are other appli-

---

11. Also shelved with the three Restatement series are "Tentative Drafts." Prior to being approved by the American Law Institute, each Restatement goes through a series of drafts. The process can take years; some drafts are never approved or are approved only in part. The drafts are published with the notation "T.D." and are occasionally cited by the courts. The second and third series include "Conversion Tables" that indicate where a section in a Tentative Draft appears in the final Restatement, assuming the draft is adopted.

cable Restatement sections. The illustrations, some of which are based on reported cases, will apply the rule to specific facts.

In addition to comments and illustrations, the Second and Third Series include Reporter's Notes for each section, which contain background information and citations to authority on which the drafters relied. Depending on the subject and series, these notes may appear in appendix volumes instead of topic volumes.

Restatements are also available on Lexis and Westlaw. In some cases, full-text searching of these databases may be more helpful than using the print versions. However, you need to understand the different components of the Restatements (black letter rules, comments, illustrations, citing cases) in either print or online formats.

C. The Role of Restatements in Research

Restatements are most often used for their black letter rules and as research tools for finding primary authority. Some situations allow you to use them as authority when writing to a court. As you research the application of your Restatement section, you may find that it has been adopted by your jurisdiction. In this case only, you can cite the Restatement as authoritative. You should cite the case that adopted the Restatement section, but you can use the Restatement as additional authority. You may also find that courts have cited a section approvingly without adopting it. In that case, you should continue to look for primary authority on point.

D. Updating and Citing Restatements

Although Restatements are published in different series, a later series does not necessarily supersede a specific rule in an earlier series. If a court in your state has adopted a certain Restatement section as the law of that state, it will continue to be the law even if a subsequent version of the Restatement omits or alters its statement of the rule, unless the same court later explicitly adopts the newer version in place of the older one.

Restatements are supplemented by a sometimes confusing system of appendix volumes along with bound and paper supplements. To thoroughly research a particular section, therefore, you will need to gather several volumes: the Restatement topic volumes, bound Appendix volumes, and any supplemental bound or paper volumes. Many researchers prefer online searching for this reason. When researching in printed Restatements, it is best to consult with a librarian.

Alternatively, Shepard's and KeyCite will allow you to determine whether any section of a Restatement has been cited by state or federal courts, or by one of a small group of law reviews. Although these services provide extensive coverage of Restatement rules, they do not include treatment codes. Courts can, among other things, adopt, reject, discuss, disapprove, or merely cite Restatement sections; you will have to check each case yourself to find the treatment. Another easy starting point for finding cases citing a particular Restatement provision is simply to search a case law database for the provision. For example, to find cases discussing section 314A of the Restatement (Second) of Torts, you might search a database of Florida cases for all decisions where "Restatement," "Torts," and "314A" appear in the same sentence.

In office memos, a Restatement section that has been adopted in your jurisdiction can be used in your analysis almost as you would use a case holding. The comments and illustrations to a section that has been adopted would be regarded as predictive of how a court would apply the section. In situations where you are asking a court to address an issue of first impression, a Restatement rule on point can be highly persuasive authority. You can also use a Restatement rule to support an argument that a prior holding should be modified or overruled according to a modern trend.

Cite Restatements by giving the title, section number, and the year in which that Restatement was adopted. The year appears on the title page of each volume, or online at the bottom of each section.

Chapter 7

Research Aids

Building on the discussion of secondary sources in Chapter 6, this chapter addresses a group of research tools that are loosely called "research aids." The two categories overlap, but secondary sources tend to include more analysis of the law and more references to primary authorities, while research aids tend to help an attorney create documents or stay current in specific legal areas. This chapter addresses legal forms, practice area services, blogs, apps, and library guides.

I. Forms

A. Purpose of Legal Forms

The purpose of a form is to offer a general model for the legal documents that lawyers frequently need to draft. By using a form, you can avoid reinventing the wheel, thus saving your time and your client's money. Legal forms include samples of documents ranging from contracts to wills or material on a particular area of law. Forms for civil pleadings might include model complaints for various causes of action, model discovery requests, and model motions. An example of a form appears in Figure 7-1; this form would be prepared by the defendant's attorney and issued by a court clerk when a defendant files a crossclaim against the plaintiff (called the "crossclaim defendant").

While you are unlikely to find a form exactly like the document you are trying to draft, forms offer a starting point for unfamiliar territory. Various sources for legal forms (in print and online) often include helpful commentary about the forms, cross references to secondary sources, explanatory notes, and checklists of information you need to complete the forms and related legal matters you should consider.

Figure 7-1. Sample Form

CROSSCLAIM SUMMONS

THE STATE OF FLORIDA:
To Each Sheriff of the State:

      YOU ARE COMMANDED to serve this summons and a copy of the crossclaim in this action on defendant ....

      Each crossclaim defendant is required to serve written defenses to the crossclaim on ...., defendant's attorney, whose address is ...., and on ...., plaintiff's attorney, whose address is ...., within 20 days after service of this summons on that defendant, exclusive of the day of service, and to file the original of the defenses with the clerk of this court either before service on the attorneys or immediately thereafter. If a crossclaim defendant fails to do so, a default will be entered against that defendant for the relief demanded in the crossclaim.

      DATED on ....

                          (Name of Clerk)
                          As Clerk of the Court

                          By _____
                          As Deputy Clerk

Source: Florida Rules of Civil Procedure, Form 1.903.

B. How to Use Legal Forms

To use forms successfully, you must research the legal issues that need to be addressed in your form, compare different possible forms, and then modify the most suitable forms to fit your specific situation.

1. Research Legal Issues

Before trying to use a form, research your legal issues and decide exactly what the final document needs to accomplish. Consult secondary sources and research primary sources. A major development in the law may render some forms obsolete or, at least, questionable.

2. Compare Forms from Different Sources

To find all relevant forms, cast a wide net in the terms you use and the resources you review. Online, use a variety of search terms and skim through several of the results. In print, most form books have a topical index to help you find a relevant form. To find appropriate forms in one of those form books, refer to your list of research terms and look for each term in the form book's index or table of contents.

Often you will need to combine elements of several forms to create an appropriate document. If you have access to several different forms, comparing forms can help you choose the best language and tailor the document to your needs or find a form more specific to your facts.

3. Understand and Edit the Form

After choosing a form, or several forms, to use, you must be sure you understand every word that you include in your document. You should not assume that the language of any form is correct. Forms are not binding authority, and one term can completely change the meaning of a document. For instance, if you are drafting a document transferring title to real property, it makes a difference whether you are transferring it to two people as joint tenants (which carries a right of survivorship) or as tenants in common (which does not).

Using a form effectively requires more than simply inserting the names of your parties. Be especially careful in using a form when the document you are drafting is heavily fact-dependent. For example, in a complaint for fraud, courts require specific factual pleadings. If you rely too heavily on a form to draft your complaint, you may not have enough facts to withstand a motion to dismiss for failure to state a cause of action.

Many forms use archaic language. Careful editing and use of plain English can greatly clarify the meaning and intent of a form. Legal writing textbooks can be helpful when you are editing a form. Be particularly careful when using forms that are available online or in a publication that is not solely for a legal audience. Although such forms may be helpful starting points, you should not use them exclusively when drafting a document for a client.

C. Sources for Locating Forms

1. Previously Drafted Documents

Probably the best way to draft a document for the first time is to pattern your document after a similar document previously drafted by a more experienced lawyer in your office. You can probably improve on the older document, but it will give you insight into your office's approach to that type of document and help you draft a document that meets your supervisor's expectations.

2. Form Books

"Form books" are unique practice aids; they contain many forms on a variety of topics. A typical property form book might have sample forms for mortgages, deeds, and documents necessary for closing a sale of real property. A list of widely recognized form books appears in Table 7-1.

Table 7-1. Selected Form Books

Florida Form Books

1. *Florida Jurisprudence Forms: Legal and Business Transactions*. These form books are divided into two main sections: pleading and practice forms, and business forms. Each of these major sections has its own index for finding specific forms.

2. *Trawick's Florida Practice and Procedure: Forms*. Because this one volume contains the most common and basic Florida forms, many practitioners include it in their libraries.

3. *Florida Legal Forms*

4. *Florida Pleading & Practice Forms*

5. *Bender's Florida Forms: Pleadings*

6. *LaCoe's Pleading Under the Florida Rules of Civil Procedure With Forms*

7. *Supreme Court Approved Simplified Forms*

8. *Legal Forms and Worksheets*

9. *Florida Will and Trust Forms Manual*

Federal Form Books

1. *West's Federal Forms*

2. *American Jurisprudence Pleading and Practice Forms Annotated*

3. *American Jurisprudence Proof of Facts*

4. *Bender's Federal Practice Forms*

5. *Federal Procedural Forms*

6. *Cyclopedia of Legal Forms Annotated*

Form Books for Specific Subjects

1. *Modern Real Estate and Mortgage Forms*

2. *Complete Manual of Criminal Forms*

3. *Bender's Forms of Discovery*

4. *Fletcher Corporation Forms, Annotated*

3. Court Rules

Some rules of court include forms adopted by the highest court of that jurisdiction. It is important to check court rules for forms because parties are often required to use the specific form as adopted by the court. For example, the Florida Supreme Court has adopted interrogatories for certain types of negligence actions. If you are representing a party in one of these cases, your first set of interrogatories must include these form interrogatories adopted by the Florida Supreme Court. See Chapter 8 for a discussion of court rules, including sources for forms included in court rules.

4. Practitioners' Publications

Many books written for practitioners include forms. For example, many publications of The Florida Bar, including Continuing Legal Education publications (and other CLE publications as well), include forms. Even when a CLE publication does not include a form, it will often include checklists for drafting pleadings, discovery requests, or motions in a particular area of law. These checklists can be even more useful than a form, especially in new or changing areas of the law.

5. Jury Instructions

Model jury instructions or, even better, jury instructions that have been approved by the Florida Supreme Court, can provide a good checklist for drafting pleadings. The Florida Bar publishes a book of court-approved jury instructions. Additionally, The Florida Bar produces computer software to help practitioners use court-approved jury instructions. Jury instructions that the Florida Supreme Court has approved are available on the court's website at www.floridasupremecourt.org/jury_instructions/instructions.shtml. Because the Florida Supreme Court approves changes to the standard jury instructions, they are also published in the *Southern Reporter* and available online.

6. Encyclopedias and Treatises

Many other secondary sources, including encyclopedias and treatises, also include sample forms. For Florida practitioners, a good source of forms is *Florida Jurisprudence Forms: Legal and Business Transactions*, which accompanies the legal encyclopedia *Florida Jurisprudence (Second)* and is available both in print and on Westlaw. Wright and Miller's *Federal Practice and Procedure* and *Moore's Federal Practice* cover rules of federal practice and include some sample forms, usually arranged by rule rather than by topic.

7. Commercial Providers

Westlaw and Lexis both have databases of forms among their secondary sources and practice materials. Both commercial providers also have databases of actual litigation pleadings from various jurisdictions.

8. Other Sources for Legal Forms

Another type of form book is a book (or set of books) that explains how to conduct a trial for a certain cause of action or what is required to prove a cause of action. One example is *American Jurisprudence Trials*, which takes the reader through model trials for various causes of action, explaining what steps should be taken for each particular cause of action. Another example of this type of form book is *American Jurisprudence Proof of Facts*, which explains the elements of proof for various causes of action. You should explore your law library and online resources to become acquainted with the various types of practice aids that are available.

II. Practice Area Services

A. Overview

Practice area services are compilations of primary and secondary materials in a specific area of the law. Some practice area services function as mini-libraries on certain topics and can include the text of statutes, regulations, court cases, and administrative agency decisions, along with commentary. Other practice area services contain current news and developments in specific practice areas.

B. Locating Practice Area Services

In general, you will locate practice area services the same way you locate treatises or practice tools. Using your library's catalog system, you can find appropriate titles using key word searches. You can also search for specific publishers and scan the list of their titles for one that might address your issue. Three of the major publishers of practice area services are Commerce Clearing House (CCH), Matthew Bender, and the Bureau of National Affairs (BNA). Westlaw carries numerous CCH publications and Lexis has Matthew Bender publications; however, the two overlap somewhat. Only Bloomberg carries BNA publications. Some examples of common practice area services are listed in Table 7-2.

Table 7-2. Examples of Practice Area Services

Topic	Title and Publisher
Bankruptcy	*Bankruptcy Law Reporter* (both BNA and CCH)
Employee Benefits	*Employee Benefits Guide* (Bender)
Environmental Law	*Environmental Reporter* (BNA)
Federal Taxation	*Standard Federal Tax Reporter* (CCH)
Immigration	*Immigration and Nationality Act Service* (Bender)
Labor Law	*Labor Relations Reporter* (BNA)
Medicare and Medicaid	*Medicare and Medicaid Guide* (CCH)

To find practice area services on Westlaw or Lexis, you can browse sources for the name of a publisher to see what is available. Alternatively, on West-lawNext, you can explore the "Topical Practice Areas" to find databases corresponding to one of the major publishers. In Lexis Advance, you can use the "Browse Sources" feature to locate practice area services libraries. Once you find a database containing material in your practice area, you will typically search the full text for relevant materials.

Some practice area services provided by other businesses are also available over the Internet, but they typically require a subscription because of the amount of work that updating a service requires. An increasing number of the services offered by major publishers are now available in web-based versions. An example of an Internet practice area service is the Environmental Law Institute's *Environmental Law Reporter*, at www.elr.info/index.cfm. This website provides links to the type of inter-related material typically found in a practice area service.

Some law school libraries provide access to BNA's practice area services without having to access the Bloomberg site. These services may be available to only students and faculty, or to all patrons physically present in the library. An example of a BNA service, the Daily Tax Report, is shown in Figure 7-2.

Figure 7-2. Example Practice Area Service

HOME   CUSTOMIZE TOPICS   MY FOLDERS   ACCOUNT PROFILE   GETTING STARTED   ABOUT   CONTACT US   HELP   SIGN

Bloomberg
BNA   **Daily Tax Report®**   Advanced Search

LATEST NEWS   KEY FEATURES   BNA INSIGHTS   RECENT TOPICS   FINDING TOOLS

☒ Sign up for/customize email updates

Welcome. Create an account profile.   LATEST ISSUE   NEWS ARCHIVE

Hot Topics   Daily Tax RealTime®

- Accounting
- Banking and Finance   **IRS Will Amend Rules for U.S. Persons Owning PFIC Stock Through**
- Corporate Reporting   **Certain Exempt Organizations**
  Requirements   Posted: Apr 14, 2014, 5:08 PM EDT
- Electronic Commerce Law
- Estate Tax   **IRS Releases Housing Cost Exclusions, Deductions Adjusted for 2014**
- Health Care   Posted: Apr 14, 2014, 2:53 PM EDT
- Sales and Use Taxes
- Tax Evasion
- Tax Legislation   **BNA Highlights** 🖨 Print Now | All Headlines | All Headlines with Summaries
- Tax Shelters
                                  Issue dated Monday, April 14, 2014 • Number 71

Recent Topics   HIGHLIGHTS
Customize
All Recent Topics ›   **Wealthiest Pay Bigger Tax Bills With Little Harm to Economy,**
                                  Analysts Say

TaxCore®   As the political fight over raising taxes for high-
Home Page   income Americans fades away, so are predictions
                                                        for negative economic fallout. The bill for President
                                                        Obama's 2013 tax increases comes due April 15,
Key Features   and the first boost in marginal income rates in 20
                                                        years is already reducing the U.S. budget deficit
NEW Key Tax Issues in Congress   without tipping the economy into recession. "In
                                                        advance one always hears the squeals of the oxen

Source: Reproduced with permission from *Daily Tax Report*. Copyright 2014 by The Bureau of National Affairs, Inc. (800-372-1033), http://www.bna.com.

C. Citing Practice Area Services

If your research in a practice area service reveals cases that are published in a reporter (or applicable sections of statutory or administrative codes), cite to the primary authorities and not the practice area service.

III. Blogs

One way to keep current on developments in an area of law is to follow a blog. For example, www.scotusblog.com closely follows developments in the United States Supreme Court. The site includes transcripts of oral arguments, in-depth analysis of cases, and even live blogging as opinions are issued. For a comprehensive list of currently updated law blogs, see www.abajournal.com/ blawgs/. The blogs are organized in several ways, including by topic. The topics listed range from the very broad, such as torts law, to the very narrow, such as Guantanamo/Detainees. Virtually every area of law is represented.

IV. Apps

Many apps for smartphones and tablets exist, including apps for Lexis Advance, WestlawNext, Bloomberg, and Fastcase. The apps are free, but you must have a subscription to use them. They work quite well and you can perform all the research functions you could from a desktop computer. Another useful app is Florida Rules, which contains links to the court websites, The Florida Bar, and rules of state and federal courts, including federal local rules.

V. LibGuides

Most Florida law schools have helpful research guides available on their library websites. These research guides, created by law librarians, are sometimes called *LibGuides* or *Pathfinders*. They contain information on how to research specific areas of the law, such as environmental law, or how to use different kinds of legal sources, such as secondary sources. For an example of a LibGuide, see Figure 7-3.

Figure 7-3. Example LibGuide

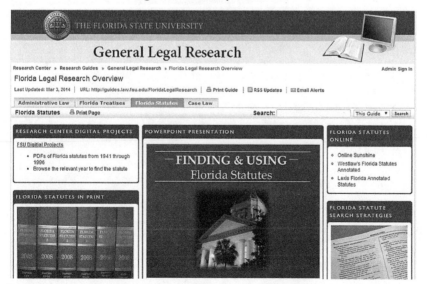

Source: Florida State College of Law Research Center, http://guides.law.fsu.edu/FloridaLegalResearch.

To find available guides, go to a library website and look for a tab such as "Research Resources" or "Research Guides." Remember that for federal sources, or for researching the law of other states, you can use LibGuides from law schools outside of Florida, such as the research guides from the Georgetown Law Library. In addition to providing background information on subject areas, LibGuides include links to useful sources, including Lexis and Westlaw, and free legal research websites. LibGuides also typically include information showing the date of the last update, so be sure to check how current a LibGuide is before relying on it.

Chapter 8

Rules of Court and Ethics

I. Introduction

Court rules govern all aspects of court proceedings. Examples of the more common court rules include rules of civil procedure, rules of criminal procedure, rules of appellate procedure, and rules of evidence. In addition, through rules of professional conduct, courts regulate the conduct of attorneys in the practice of law. These rules address the relationships of attorneys with clients, opposing counsel, the court, and others.

Separate court rules govern state and federal courts. In addition, procedural rules exist at several levels, so practitioners in most jurisdictions need to be aware of a combination of court rules. These include rules that have been promulgated at the highest level and are applicable in all courts, as well as *local rules* that have been promulgated by individual courts for practitioners appearing in those courts. Together, these rules of procedure guide decisions at all stages of litigation. The Florida Rules of Civil Procedure, for example, govern such things as which parties may be joined in a civil action, when summary judgment is appropriate, and what grounds will justify imposing sanctions on attorneys. Court rules also govern more mundane aspects of litigation, such as filing procedure and payment of fees, mandatory pre-trial conferences, and even paper size for documents submitted to the court.[1] While format requirements may be mundane, they are nevertheless important because courts may refuse to accept documents that do not comply. An example of a court rule is provided in Table 8-1.

---

1. *See, e.g.*, Fla. R. App. P. 2.10(a)(2).

Table 8-1. Example of Court Rule

Florida Rule of Judicial Administration 2.516(b)(1):

All documents required or permitted to be served on another party must be served by e-mail, unless the parties otherwise stipulate or this rule otherwise provides. A filer of an electronic document has complied with this subdivision if the Florida Courts e-filing Portal ("Portal") or other authorized electronic filing system with a supreme court approved electronic service system ("e-Service system") served the document by e-mail or provided a link by e-mail to the document on a website maintained by a clerk ("e-Service"). The filer of an electronic document must verify that the Portal or other e-Service system uses the names and e-mail addresses provided by the parties pursuant to subdivision (b)(1)(A).

Court rules cannot conflict with statutes, or give parties greater or fewer rights than are available under applicable substantive law.[2] Even with that limitation, court rules can often affect the availability of a substantive remedy, and rules have the force of law within the jurisdiction where they are promulgated. Therefore, whenever you begin work on a project that will involve taking some action in court, you should determine which rules of court apply. For example, if a lawyer files a complaint, but does not include the filing fee, the court might not consider the complaint timely filed until the filing fee is included. This delay could create statute of limitations problems.

II. Researching Florida Rules of Court

Article V, section 2 of the Florida Constitution gives the Florida Supreme Court authority to adopt rules of practice and procedure for all Florida courts. Florida has rules of court for many areas, including those set out in Table 8-2.

---

2. *See* 28 U.S.C. § 2072.

Table 8-2. Florida Court Rules

Florida Rules of Civil Procedure

Florida Rules of Appellate Procedure

Florida Rules of Criminal Procedure

Florida Evidence Code

Florida Rules of Judicial Administration

Florida Rules of Traffic Court

Florida Small Claims Rules

Florida Rules of Juvenile Procedure

Florida Family Law Rules of Procedure

Rules Regulating The Florida Bar

A. Finding the Text of Florida Rules of Court

Florida court rules are published in many formats. *Florida Statutes Annotated* (FSA) publishes Florida Rules of Court in its last volumes. Use the detailed table of contents at the beginning of each set of rules to locate a specific rule on point, and then read annotations of cases that have applied or interpreted the rule. The rules are also available in the first three volumes of LexisNexis's *Florida Rules of Court Annotated*. The official statutory compilation, *Florida Statutes*, does not include the rules.

A handy print source for rules that many lawyers use is a deskbook that compiles the court rules for the lawyer's jurisdiction. West publishes a deskbook for each state with rules of court for that state. These deskbooks usually include some of the notes from the drafters of the rules, but little or no case annotations or commentary. *Florida Rules of Court: Volume I — State* contains all the sets of rules mentioned in Table 8-2 and some less well known rules. The Florida Bar's Continuing Legal Education Division publishes Florida court rules in paperback. These and other sources contain not only the rules, but also accompanying forms that are approved or mandated by the Florida Supreme Court.

Because the Florida Supreme Court has rule-making authority for the Florida court system, amendments to court rules are submitted to the Florida Supreme Court for approval. When the court approves the amendments, they are published

Table 8-3. Websites for Florida State and Federal Courts

State Courts		
Florida State Courts	www.flcourts.org	This is the official website of the Florida state court system and provides links to state courts at all levels.
Federal Courts		
U.S. Courts	www.uscourts.gov	This site has information about federal courts serving Florida, including local rules and internal operating procedures.
Eleventh Circuit Court of Appeals	www.ca11.uscourts.gov	
Northern District of Florida	www.flnd.uscourts.gov	
Middle District of Florida	www.flmd.uscourts.gov	
Southern District of Florida	www.flsd.uscourts.gov	

as Florida Supreme Court opinions. These opinions appear in *Florida Law Weekly* (FLW) and then later in *Southern Reporter*. The amendments are incorporated into the publications listed above according to the publishers' schedules.

Florida rules can be accessed easily on either Westlaw or Lexis. Florida rules of court can also be accessed online for free, but without annotations, at the website of The Florida Bar at www.floridabar.org. Use the "Rules" link at the top of the home page to view rules and proposed amendments to the rules, as well as a link to the Florida Supreme Court website for locating decisions involving court rules.

B. Interpreting Specific Florida Rules of Court

Finding a rule of court that addresses your issue may be just the beginning of the research process. Although some rules do not require interpretation, such as those setting out filing deadlines or brief formats, others cannot fully be understood without reading cases that have applied them.

Many sources provide information for case law and commentary interpreting Florida rules of court. As noted above, *Florida Statutes Annotated* includes the rules of court in the last volumes, along with historical notes, committee notes, cross references to related statutes and rules, citations to law review articles, library references, and annotations to case law. The pocket part or paper supplement will provide the most recent information.

Treatises are often helpful sources for material interpreting court rules. For example, *LaCoe's Pleadings Under the Florida Rules of Civil Procedure With Forms* includes the text of each rule followed by some commentary and extensive case annotations. *Ehrhardt's Florida Evidence* provides the text of each rule, commentary, and extensive citations regarding Florida's evidence rules. Similar publications are available for other Florida court rules.

Florida cases dealing with rules of court are included with other Florida cases in *Southern Reporter*. You could conduct an online search in the full text of cases (using the rule number as a search term) or search the Descriptive-Word Index in *Florida Digest 2d* for references to cases on point. Before publication in *Southern Reporter*, these cases are available in FLW. Cases are listed according to the rule they interpret at the end of the "Table of Statutes Construed" in the index of FLW. You could also check the topical index of cases in FLW under such headings as "Civil Procedure."

C. Florida Ethics

Florida professional ethics for lawyers are governed by the Rules of Professional Conduct, Chapter 4 of the Rules Regulating The Florida Bar. The Rules of Professional Conduct are based on the Model Rules of Professional Conduct, drafted by the American Bar Association, which are the basis for rules regulating lawyers in a majority of jurisdictions. Judges are governed by the Code of Judicial Conduct. These rules are included in volume 35 of *Florida Statutes Annotated*. They are also included in the West deskbook, *Florida Rules of Court: Volume I—State*.

The Preamble to the Rules of Professional Conduct notes the lawyer's three concurrent roles as representative of clients, officer of the court, and citizen with special responsibilities. The rules then delineate requirements and prohibitions for a lawyer's conduct in fulfilling these obligations. For example, the rules require that lawyers work to expedite litigation and prohibit filing frivolous claims. The rules cover relationships with clients, other parties, opposing counsel, witnesses, and the court. Of special importance as you prepare documents for a court is Rule 4-3.3, which specifically requires a lawyer to disclose controlling legal authority that is adverse to the lawyer's client and not disclosed by the opposing side.

Official comments accompanying the rules further explain the rules. For example, Rule 4-5.2 states that a lawyer working as a subordinate for another lawyer is bound by the professional conduct rules, but does not violate the rules by complying with a supervisory lawyer's reasonable resolution of an arguable question. The comment to that rule gives an example and explains various scenarios.

The Rules of Professional Conduct and Code of Judicial Conduct set high standards for the practice of law and the conduct of judges. Canon 2 of the Code of Judicial Conduct requires judges to avoid even the appearance of impropriety.

The Florida Bar website, www.floridabar.org, can be a helpful starting point for research into Florida ethical rules. In addition to the Rules Regulating The Florida Bar, the website provides links to the text of ethics opinions dating back to 1959, frequently asked ethics questions, and a list of reference sources to use when researching ethics questions.

Also, because Florida's rules are patterned after ABA model rules, ABA resources can be helpful in researching ethical issues. The ABA issues both formal and informal opinions on ethics subjects. While neither of these types of opinions is binding authority, both are persuasive in states that have patterned their ethics codes after the ABA's model rules. The model rules, with commentary, and ABA Formal Ethics Opinions are available on the website of the ABA Center for Professional Responsibility, www.abanet.org/cpr. Treatises on legal ethics can also be helpful along with the *Restatement (Third) of the Law Governing Lawyers* (2000).

III. Researching Federal Rules of Court

Congress has the power to make rules of procedure for the federal courts. However, Congress delegated rulemaking authority to the United States Supreme Court in the Rules Enabling Act of 1934. The Supreme Court first adopted the Federal Rules of Civil Procedure in 1938 under the authority of the 1934 act.[3] The Federal Rules of Civil Procedure apply to cases litigated in

---

3. In 2007, the Federal Rules of Civil Procedure were revised stylistically, though their meaning remained unchanged. *See* Lisa Eichhorn, *Clarity and the Federal Rules of Civil Procedure: A Lesson from the Style Project,* http://www.alwd.org/lcr/archives/fall-2008/eichhorn/.

federal district courts. Rule 83 allows each district court to promulgate its own local rules, so long as those rules do not conflict with the Federal Rules of Civil Procedure. A similar combination of rules applies to cases at the appellate level. The Federal Rules of Appellate Procedure apply to all federal circuits; each circuit also has its own local rules as well as internal operating procedures (IOPs).

A. Finding the Text of Federal Rules of Court

The *United States Code, United States Code Annotated*, and *United States Code Service* all include federal court rules. In the *United States Code*, the Federal Rules of Civil Procedure, Federal Rules of Appellate Procedure, Federal Rules of Evidence, and other less commonly used rules are found in the volume containing Title 28 on the Judiciary and Judicial Procedure. The rules are located in an appendix at the end of Title 28. Similarly, the Federal Rules of Criminal Procedure are found in an appendix following Title 18 on Crimes and Criminal Procedure.

In the *United States Code Annotated* (USCA), these rules also follow Title 28 and Title 18 respectively, but the rules are in special rules volumes. In the *United States Code Service* (USCS), rules are in special Court Rules volumes at the end of the series. Both USCA and USCS contain local rules of the federal circuits. In both USCA and USCS, be sure to check for pocket parts and supplemental paper volumes for current information.

West's *Federal Civil Judicial Procedure and Rules* includes the Federal Rules of Civil Procedure, Federal Rules of Evidence, Federal Rules of Appellate Procedure, and some federal statutes dealing with jurisdiction and procedure. Other deskbooks for federal rules also exist, such as *Moore's Federal Rules Pamphlet*. Use the index or table of contents for these sources to find the relevant rule or rules for your project.

West deskbooks for each state include a companion volume containing rules for the federal courts located in that state. West's *Florida Rules of Court: Volume II—Federal* contains Federal Rules of Evidence, Federal Rules of Appellate Procedure (including Eleventh Circuit Rules and Internal Operating Procedures) and local rules for the federal district courts (including Bankruptcy Courts) sitting in Florida. Other information in the federal deskbook includes fee schedules for the various courts.

Local rules are available in *Federal Local Court Rules*. You could also obtain local rules of federal courts directly from the court clerk or from the court website. (See Table 8-3 earlier in this chapter.)

B. Interpreting Specific Federal Rules of Court

As noted regarding Florida rules, you may need to do further research to determine how a rule should be interpreted and applied in your case. Most federal rules include advisory comments to help in interpreting the rules. These comments show what the drafters of the rule had in mind when they wrote the rule. Remember that these comments are not binding authority, but they are very persuasive.

One key way to interpret rules is to find case law that has applied the specific rule you have found. There are several ways to find citations to relevant cases. You can use USCA and USCS to find case annotations as well as advisory committee notes and research aids on each rule. You can also Shepardize or KeyCite the rule.

Cases interpreting the rules are available through services such as *Federal Rules Service*, which indexes and reports decisions regarding the Federal Rules of Civil Procedure and the Federal Rules of Appellate Procedure. The *Federal Rules of Evidence Service* does the same for the Federal Rules of Evidence. The advantages of using a service are that services are often more current than any other source, and some cases are not published anywhere else. Because these are West publications, they are also available on Westlaw. On Lexis, the USCS Federal Rules Annotated database would be one starting point for research into the federal rules.

Another source that can explain the rules of court is a treatise. The footnotes in treatises contain references to cases on point. Treatises exist for each set of federal court rules. Use your library's catalog and scan the stacks to find treatises on point. There are many well respected treatises written on the federal rules of procedure. Among the most widely recognized are Wright and Miller's *Federal Practice and Procedure* and *Moore's Federal Practice*. While these are based on treatises written years ago, they are kept current by professors and practitioners. Some other treatises include *Cyclopedia of Federal Procedure*, *Federal Procedure, Lawyers' Edition*, and *West's Federal Practice Manual*. An especially helpful treatise on evidence is *Weinstein's Federal Evidence*.

After finding citations to case law interpreting federal rules, you can find the cases in reporters or online. One source for these cases is the West reporter called *Federal Rules Decisions* (FRD). FRD reports federal court decisions regarding rules of civil and criminal procedure and includes commentary articles. Opinions appearing in FRD that address only procedures or rules will not appear in any other West case law reporters. Decisions involving both procedural and substantive issues, however, will also appear in *Federal Supplement* or *Federal Reporter*.

Chapter 9

Citation

I. The Purpose of Citation

Lawyers often use the results of legal research in documents that explain the legal analysis of a client's problem to another lawyer. Law clerks and junior attorneys frequently write office memoranda to senior attorneys, explaining the law and showing how it applies to the client's legal issue. In a brief submitted to a court, an attorney explains why the law favors the outcome desired by the client.

When you write a legal document, you must include citations to the legal authority that you found in your research and relied upon in your analysis. Your citations will include both the name of the authority and where it is published. You need to communicate this information with precision so that the reader can easily find and verify the authority supporting your analysis.

This chapter begins by introducing the three citation systems most Florida lawyers encounter, as well as the *Florida Style Manual*. Then the chapter explains correct citation of cases and statutes, the use of signals, and frequent citation errors.

II. Citation for Florida Attorneys

There are numerous systems for citing legal authority, but the basic information required for all legal citations is consistent from one system to another. Often the citations resulting from different citation systems are similar if not identical. This chapter provides guidance on three sources of legal citation forms: Rule 9.800 of the Florida Rules of Appellate Procedure, the *Bluebook*,[1]

---

1. *The Bluebook: A Uniform System of Citation* (Columbia Law Review Ass'n et al. eds., 19th ed. 2010).

and the *ALWD Guide*.[2] When practicing in Florida, you should follow Rule 9.800 and supplement it with one of the other sources. A student working for a professor or writing for law journals should use the citation system they prefer. After mastering one system, adjusting to another system is not difficult.

A. Florida Rule 9.800

To ensure uniformity in citation, lawyers in Florida follow Florida Rule of Appellate Procedure 9.800.[3] That rule includes citation forms that must be used in documents submitted to Florida appellate courts. In practice, most lawyers in Florida follow Rule 9.800 in all formal documents, even in internal office memoranda that will not be submitted to a court. As discussed below, Rule 9.800 citation forms for certain authorities differ from the forms required under the *Bluebook* or *ALWD Guide*.

Rule 9.800 provides minimal explanation, but gives examples of proper citations for most legal authority specific to Florida. You should follow Rule 9.800 as the primary authority for citations unless instructed otherwise. The following sections of Rule 9.800 are the ones you will likely use the most.

Florida Supreme Court cases: Rule 9.800(a)
   Smallwood v. State, 113 So. 3d 724 (Fla. 2013).

Florida District Court of Appeal cases: Rule 9.800(b)
   Harris v. Soha, 15 So. 3d 767 (Fla. 1st DCA 2009).

Florida statutes: Rule 9.800(f)
   § 92.57, Fla. Stat. (2013).

Florida administrative and court rules: Rule 9.800(i)
   Fla. R. Crim. P. 3.850.

Federal cases: Rule 9.800(k), (l), and (m)
   Black Warrior Riverkeeper, Inc. v. Black Warrior Minerals, Inc., 734 F.3d 1297 (11th Cir. 2013).

---

2. Association of Legal Writing Directors & Coleen M. Barger, *ALWD Guide to Legal Citation* (5th ed. 2014) (previously *ALWD Citation Manual: A Professional System of Citation*).

3. Florida Rules of Appellate Procedure are widely available online. One source is the website of The Florida Bar, using the "Rules" link on the home page.

Rule 9.800 does not provide citation forms for citing materials from other jurisdictions. Also, it is not detailed enough to contain information about standard abbreviations or other conventions typically used by practitioners and scholars. Therefore, although the Rule is the best starting point when writing for a Florida audience, you will have to supplement Rule 9.800 with citation conventions from other sources. Rule 9.800(o) refers specifically to the *Bluebook* and the *Florida Manual of Style* (discussed below) for additional citation guidance.

B. The *Bluebook*

The *Bluebook* is compiled by the editors of law reviews at four elite schools. The editors' goal is to provide a uniform system of citation for articles published in their law reviews, regardless of the citation rules of the states where authors of various articles work. The *Bluebook* contains almost 500 pages of instructions. It covers in detail not only which source to cite and how to abbreviate the source, but also minor technicalities like the spacing between the letters of the abbreviation. Because of its size and complexity, the *Bluebook* is daunting at first. With practice, however, it can become a helpful tool.

Because the *Bluebook* is written by members of law journals, most of the examples provided are in the form used by law journals.[4] These forms evolved before personal computers made different typefaces widely available for practitioners; because law reviews were professionally typeset, they were able to use a wider variety of typefaces. For example, a cite to *Florida Statutes* in a law journal requires use of large and small capital letters: Fla. Stat. In an office memorandum or appellate brief, the abbreviation would use only initial capital letters: Fla. Stat.

The "Bluepages" at the front of the *Bluebook* explain how to translate the examples given for law journals into citations for other documents. The Bluepages and the quick reference table inside the back cover are the only examples in the *Bluebook* for citing material in documents other than law journals. Thus, using the *Bluebook* requires a two-step process: first, determine the content of your citation, using the applicable *Bluebook* rule or rules; then, convert

---

4. The placement of citations differs between law journals and other legal documents. In law journals, citations are placed in footnotes at the bottom of the page. In most office memoranda, court briefs, and other documents, citations are placed in the text, immediately following the information or idea cited. The examples given in this chapter are in the style used by practitioners.

it to the appropriate typeface using the Bluepages. Alternatively, you might try to construct your citation as much as possible using just the Bluepages, then turn to the additional rules for details not covered in the Bluepages.

While the table of contents at the front of the *Bluebook* provides some assistance in locating information, the index is invaluable. The pages noted in the index in black type give citation instructions; the pages noted in blue type give citation examples. When you find helpful information in the *Bluebook* (including the index), flag it so that you can locate it again easily.

The following pages are typically those referred to most often:

Abbreviations for months: page 444 (Table T12)
Abbreviations for periodicals: pages 444–67 (Table T13)
Abbreviations of case names: pages 430–31 (Table T6)
Bluepages: pages 3–51
Case names: pages 89–95 (Rule 10.2)
Citation to articles: pages 147–51 (Rule 16)
Citation to statutes: pages 114–16 (Rule 12.3)
Explanatory parentheticals: pages 12 and 100–02
Federal materials: pages 215–28 (Table T1)
Florida materials: page 237 (Table T1)
Quotations: pages 76–79 (Rule 5)
Signals: pages 5–7 and 54–56 (Rule 1.2)
Spacing: page 80 (Rule 6.1)

C. The *ALWD Guide*

The *ALWD Guide to Legal Citation* is written by legal writing professionals.[5] First published in 2000 as the *ALWD Citation Manual*, the *ALWD Guide* covers citation for both law review articles and practice documents with a single set of citation rules.

The citation form resulting from following the *Bluebook* and the *ALWD Guide* are identical. Most novices, however, find using the *ALWD Guide* much easier because of its clear instructions and examples and its use of a single set of rules.

---

5. The lead author is Professor Coleen Barger of the University of Arkansas at Little Rock Bowen School of Law.

Both the table of contents and the index are helpful for finding information in the *ALWD Guide*. Example citations are given at the beginning of many chapters in "Fast Formats" charts.

D. The *Florida Style Manual*

The *Florida Style Manual* (FSM) is published every few years by the *Florida State University Law Review*. It covers citation to specific Florida authority not addressed by Rule 9.800, the *Bluebook*, or the *ALWD Guide*. Because the FSM is an outgrowth of the law review's Legislative Review issue, the sources included in the FSM are often related to legislative history. For example, the FSM provides abbreviations for Florida legislative committees that should be used in citing state legislative history material. The FSM is available online.

III. Case Citation

Each full citation to a reported case must convey the following information: (1) the name of the case; (2) the volume of the reporter in which the case is published, the abbreviation of the reporter, the page number on which the case begins, and the specific page that supports your point; (3) the geographic jurisdiction where the case was decided and the court that decided the case; and (4) the date the case was decided.

A. Case Name

Cite only the first party listed on each side of the case, and use only surnames for individuals. When cases are cited in footnotes or in citation sentences, words listed in specific tables (e.g., Table T6 of the *Bluebook*) can be abbreviated. When case names appear in textual sentences, avoid abbreviations.

Be aware that the case names noted at the top of each page in a case reporter are not necessarily in correct Florida, *Bluebook*, or *ALWD* form. Use the name noted at the top of each page in the reporter only as a starting point for building your own citation.

B. Reporter Volume and Page

Even cases retrieved from online websites are cited by reference to their print reporters. Cases from the Florida Supreme Court and from the Florida District Courts of Appeal are cited to the *Southern Reporter*, a West reporter. The second series of this reporter is abbreviated as So. 2d, and the third series is abbreviated as So. 3d; note that "So." by itself indicates a case that was published in the first series. In Florida, if a case is so recent it does not have a citation in the *Southern Reporter*, then it is cited to the *Florida Law Weekly* (FLW).

Cases from federal district courts are reported in *Federal Supplement*, abbreviated F. Supp., now in its second series, which is abbreviated F. Supp. 2d. Cases from the Eleventh Circuit are reported in *Federal Reporter*, which is abbreviated F., F.2d, or F.3d, depending on the date of the case. Federal decisions concerning federal rules of civil and criminal procedure that do not appear in *Federal Supplement* are reported in *Federal Rules Decisions*, abbreviated as F.R.D.[6] United States Supreme Court cases are most often cited to *United States Reports* (U.S.), the official reporter, or *Supreme Court Reporter* (S. Ct.), a West publication.

A case citation must include the reporter volume number, found on the spine of each volume (or preceding the reporter abbreviation in an online citation). Following the volume number and reporter abbreviation, give the page on which the case begins. In most instances, also include the exact page that contains the information you are citing. This page is called the "pinpoint" cite (also called the "pincite" or the "jump" cite). A pinpoint cite is especially helpful in locating information in lengthy cases, but you should include a pinpoint citation whenever possible. In the following example, the case begins on page 1297, but the relevant information appears on page 1299.

Example: *Black Warrior Riverkeeper, Inc. v. Black Warrior Minerals, Inc.*, 734 F.3d 1297, 1299 (11th Cir. 2013).

If the portion of the opinion you are citing appears on the first page of the reported case, repeat that page number in your full citation. Remember, however, that editorial aids such as headnotes should never be cited.

Ensuring correct pinpoint citation can be difficult when working with online documents. An asterisk will indicate in the text where the reporter volume has turned from one page to the next. Thus, for the *Black Warrior* example above, the idea being cited followed the notation *1299 in the text of the opinion. If a case is reported in more than one reporter, the pinpoint citations in different reporters may be indicated by the number of asterisks preceding the page num-

---

6. Only a small percentage of the cases decided by federal courts are reported in official reporters. Before relying on an "unpublished" decision or citing it to a court, be sure you know whether the jurisdiction in which you are practicing has any rules regarding the use of such opinions. See Chapter 2, Judicial Opinions, for more discussion of how to find and cite unpublished opinions.

bers. A Supreme Court case might have one asterisk before pinpoint pages in *United States Reports,* two asterisks before the pinpoint pages in *Supreme Court Reporter,* and so on. The more advanced online services, however, let you select a single reporter and display only its pagination.

C. Jurisdiction and Court

A parenthetical after the reporter abbreviation and page number includes the jurisdiction, court, and date of the decision. For Florida state cases, the jurisdiction notation in the parenthetical is Fla., indicating that the case was decided by a Florida state court.[7]

If the case was decided by the Florida Supreme Court, no court abbreviation is needed; the legal reader assumes that when no court abbreviation is given the case is from the highest court in the jurisdiction. If the case was decided by one of the district courts of appeal, note which one. For example, the parenthetical (Fla. 2d DCA 2006) indicates that the Second District Court of Appeal decided the case.

The requirement in Rule 9.800(b)(1) to identify the specific district court of appeal that decided a case differs from *Bluebook* and *ALWD* requirements, as do the abbreviations used for the different district courts. The requirement in Rule 9.800 ensures that the reader knows which district court decided a case, and thus conveys the case's precedential value. Always use this form when citing a case within Florida.

For cases from federal courts sitting in Florida, use the following abbreviations:[8]

S.D. Fla.	Southern District of Florida
M.D. Fla.	Middle District of Florida
N.D. Fla.	Northern District of Florida
11th Cir.	Eleventh Circuit Court of Appeals

---

7. In some situations, the name of the reporter clearly indicates the jurisdiction in which the case was decided. For example, a case reported in *United States Reports* (U.S.) was decided by the United States Supreme Court. Because the *Southern Reporter* includes cases from four states—Florida, Alabama, Mississippi, and Louisiana—always indicate in the parenthetical that the case was decided by a Florida court.

8. Not all states have multiple districts for federal district courts. For a state that has only one district, the correct abbreviation is D. plus the appropriate state abbreviation. An example is "D. Kan."

Examples: *Ball v. D'Lites Enter., Inc.*, 65 So. 3d 637, 641 (Fla. 4th DCA
2011).
   • Jurisdiction is Florida
   • Court is the Fourth District Court of Appeal

Bush v. Schiavo, 885 So. 2d 321, 331–32 (Fla. 2004).
   • Jurisdiction is Florida
   • Court is the Florida Supreme Court

Ledford v. Delta Airlines, Inc., 658 F. Supp. 540, 542 (S.D.
Fla. 1987).
   • Jurisdiction is federal
   • Court is the federal Southern District of Florida

D. Date

The citation generally includes only the year the case was decided. Give the
exact date (month, day, and year) only in limited circumstances, including
the citation of slip opinions, decisions appearing in *Florida Law Weekly*, and
cases available only online. Do not give the date the case was argued or the
date of subsequent requests for rehearings, even if those items are included in
the case heading.

E. Use of Full Citations

The first time that you name a case, give its full citation, including all the
information outlined above. The following cite is correct but not preferred because it wastes valuable sentence space with a citation.

In *Levin, Middlebrooks, Mabie, Thomas, Mayes & Mitchell, P.A. v. U.S.
Fire Insurance Co.*, 639 So. 2d 606, 607 (Fla. 1994), the Florida Supreme
Court held that statements made during judicial proceedings were ab-
solutely privileged.

Instead of the name, consider beginning the sentence with other useful information that will not require the full citation, such as the key issue, the date,
or the name of the court. The next example keeps the unwieldy citation out
of the sentence.

Statements made during a judicial proceeding are absolutely privileged
and cannot be the basis for a tort claim. *Levin, Middlebrooks, Mabie,
Thomas, Mayes & Mitchell, P.A. v. U.S. Fire Ins. Co.*, 639 So. 2d 606,
607 (Fla. 1994).

F. Short Citation Forms for Cases

After giving the complete case citation once, use a "short" citation form that gives just enough information for the reader to find the cited material.[9] Short cites use only one party's name. Generally, use the first party's name that is listed; however, if that party is a common litigant (for example, the State of Florida), then use the opposing party's name for the short cite. Thus, in the case *State v. Jones*, the short cite name would be *Jones*, not *State*.

If the short cite refers to a different page number from the previous cite, include "at" and the pinpoint cite.[10] Short cites do not include the first page of the case (unless the pinpoint citation happens to be the first page), or the jurisdiction, court, and date parenthetical.

The following list shows the various short forms that can be used for the case *Delmonico v. Traynor*, 116 So. 3d 1205, 1219 (Fla. 2013).

> *Delmonico*, 116 So. 3d at 1219.
> 116 So. 3d at 1219.
> *Id.* at 1219.
> *Id.*

The short forms listed above do not need to be used in the order given. The only requirement is that the citation clearly indicate to the reader which source is being cited. Table 9-1 demonstrates the use of full and short cites.

Note that *id.* cannot be used when the previous citation sentence contains more than one cite because the reader will not automatically know which source is being cited again. Thus, if a sentence were to be added after the final sentence of the sample memo in Table 9-1, *id.* would be an inappropriate short form to use.

Most citations are given in citation sentences that are separated from the text by periods. A citation sentence indicates that the cited authority supports

---

9. In a lengthy document, however, you should repeat the full citation if the reader might have trouble locating it quickly. For example, you might repeat the full citation the first time you refer to a case in each part of the document: if you cite a case in full on page 5 of a brief to support your first argument, you should give the full cite again on page 12 when you refer to the same case to support your second argument.

10. Do not include "at" in full case citations. The following citation is wrong: *Delmonico v. Traynor*, 116 So. 3d 1205, at 1219 (Fla. 2013). Also incorrect is the following hybrid short form: *Delmonico* at 1219.

Table 9-1. Memo Excerpt with Full and Short Cites

	An absolute privilege shields litigants and their attorneys from tort claims based on statements made in the course of a judicial proceeding, but an attorney's ex parte, out-of-court statements enjoy only a qualified privilege.
Full cite with pinpoint ———————➤	*Delmonico v. Traynor*, 116 So. 3d 1205, 1219 (Fla. 2013). In *Delmonico*, an attorney told several potential witnesses that the plaintiff had obtained business for a marine services company by sup-
Short cite to different pages of the ➤ same case	plying prostitutes to his customers. *Id.* at 1209-10. Statements about a lawsuit made to the press, whether online or in print, are also subject to a qualified
Full cite to new case, following a ——➤ "*See*" signal	privilege. *See Ball v. D'Lites Enter., Inc.*, 65 So. 3d 637, 641 (Fla. 4th DCA 2011). A plaintiff can overcome a qualified privilege with evidence that the statements were made with express malice.
Short cite to case cited earlier. ——➤	*E.g., Delmonico*, 116 So. 3d at 1220. These decisions require attorneys to be cautious when discussing potential claims outside of court, even if litigation
Short cite to the immediately pre- ——➤ ceding case, followed by a "*see also*" signal and explanatory parenthetical	is already pending. *See id.; see also Lan-Chile Airlines v. Conn. Gen. Life Ins. Co.*, 731 F. Supp. 477, 480 (S.D. Fla. 1990) (applying Florida law to allow tort claims based on statements made before a lawsuit was filed).

the entire text sentence that precedes it. If the citation supports only part of a sentence, place the cite directly after the information it supports. These citations are called "citation clauses" and are separated from the text by commas.

> Example: The litigation privilege is 400 years old, *id.* at 1211, and balances the public interest in protecting zealous advocacy with the individual's right to maintain his or her reputation, *id.* at 1217.

This example indicates that the information about the age of the litigation privilege is found on page 1211, and information about the rationale underlying the privilege is found on page 1217.

IV. Citing Statutes

Rule 9.800, the *Bluebook*, and the *ALWD Guide* contain a few different requirements for citing Florida statutes. In general, follow Rule 9.800 when the other two conflict with it.

Rule 9.800 requires citation to *Florida Statutes*, the official codification of statutes in Florida. Follow the format of Rule 9.800(f) when citing Florida statutes to Florida courts, even though it varies slightly from that of the national citation manuals.

Examples: Rule 9.800   §95.11(4)(b), Fla. Stat. (2013).
            Bluebook and *ALWD*   Fla. Stat. §95.11(4)(b) (2013).

Under Rule 9.800(h), if the statutory language has not yet been incorporated into *Florida Statutes*, cite to *Laws of Florida*. However, if the material does not appear in *Florida Statutes*, but does appear in *Florida Statutes Annotated*, some lawyers prefer to cite to FSA.[11] In principle, the only time you would cite to FSA is when you are citing information, such as an explanatory note, that does not appear in the official statutes. When citing to FSA, indicate in the date parenthetical whether the material appears in the main volume or in the supplemental pocket part.

Always spell out the word "section" whenever it appears at the beginning of a sentence. To give the complete citation of a Florida statute in a text sentence, write out "section" and "Florida Statutes" instead of using symbols or abbreviations.[12]

Example: Section 95.11, Florida Statutes (2013), provides the statute
            of limitations for various claims in Florida. Under section
            95.11(4)(b), no claim for medical malpractice can be brought
            after two years from the alleged malpractice, except in limited
            situations involving minors.

---

11. Remember that not all bills are codified; sometimes you will have to cite to *Laws of Florida*.

12. Under the FSM, "section" should always be written out in text. Consult the citation manual you are using to determine when using the section symbol is appropriate.

V. Signals

If the cited authority clearly stands for the proposition stated in the text, no signal is needed. Using no signal indicates the citation provides the strongest support for your argument.

Otherwise, use a signal to introduce the citation and tell the reader the relevance of the cite. One of the most common signals is "*see*" — it tells the reader that the case or other authority being cited offers indirect support for the idea in the sentence.

Another frequently used signal is "*see also*" — it is used after the primary support for your idea and introduces a citation that offers additional support. Use a parenthetical after the citation to tell the reader how the citation assists in making your point, as shown in Table 9-1.

A helpful signal is "*e.g.*" — it tells the reader that more cases support your point, but listing them would merely take up space because they all say essentially the same thing. "*E.g.*" allows you to cite to just one of those cases while notifying the reader that much more support exists. It can be combined with other signals, such as "*see.*"

VI. Frequent Points of Error

The details required to cite legal authority can seem overwhelming at first. The following list highlights how to avoid some of the more common errors among those learning legal citation. The examples demonstrate the points raised in the bullets above them.

• Use a lower case v. between the parties' names.

• Do not insert a period after So. 2d or So. 3d in citing to *Southern Reporter*.

• Do not italicize (or underline) the comma separating the case name from the citation.

Example with italics:
Fladell v. Labarga, 775 So. 2d 987 (Fla. 4th DCA 2000).

Example with underlining:
Fladell v. Labarga, 775 So. 2d 987 (Fla. 4th DCA 2000).

• Always italicize (or underline) the period after *id.*

• Only capitalize *id.* when it begins a citation sentence, that is, when it is not preceded by a signal or used in a citation clause.

• When using underlining instead of italics, follow these rules: Do not underline the space between signals and case names. Also, because *id.* replaces a case name, do not underline the space between a signal and *id.* However, use a continuous line under "*see also*" and other signals containing more than one word. (The rules are the same for underlining and using italics, but italicized blanks are not apparent.)

Examples with underlining:

> See Fladell, 775 So. 2d at 989.
> See id. at 998.
> See generally Martinello v. B & P USA, Inc., 566 So. 2d 761, 763 (Fla. 1990).
> Id. at 764.

• If the idea you are citing appears on more than one page, your pinpoint citation will include all of the relevant pages. Generally, repeat only the last two digits of the page numbers.

Examples: *Delmonico,* 116 So. 3d at 1217, 1219.
          Fladell, 775 So. 2d at 989–90.

• When citing more than one case for the same point, separate the citations with a semi-colon. Do not repeat the signal if it applies to more than one case.

• Do not capitalize a signal unless it begins a citation sentence. Pay careful attention to whether a comma is needed between the signal and the citation.

Example: *Ball,* 65 So. 2d at 639; *see generally Delmonico v. Traynor,* 116 So. 3d 1205, 1211–14 (Fla. 2013) (discussing the history of the common law litigation privilege).

• In general, leave no space between consecutive abbreviations of one letter. If either abbreviation has more than one letter, include a space. For this rule, numbers combined with letters, such as 2d, 3d, or 4th, are considered single letters. One exception to this spacing rule is the court designation required by Rule 9.800 for Florida's district courts of appeal (e.g., 4th DCA).

Examples: F.3d
          So. 2d
          F. Supp.
          N.D. Fla.

- When case names appear in citations, as opposed to text sentences, abbreviate all words that appear in *Bluebook* Table T6 or *ALWD* Appendix 3(E).

- Follow Rule 9.800 for the court parenthetical following the citation of district court cases, which differs slightly from the *Bluebook* and the *ALWD Guide* (Fla. Dist. Ct. App.).

- Insert a space between two parentheticals.

    Example: *See Fladell v. Labarga*, 775 So. 2d 987 (Fla. 4th DCA 2000) (per curiam).

- Do not use italics and underlining in the same document. Choose one method, and then use that method consistently within your document.

VII. Conclusion

Using proper citation form gives documents a professional appearance. The reader can locate the authority on which you base your analysis and verify the accuracy of your work. Sloppy citation tends to make a reader less willing to rely on your work. If you do not even cite a page number correctly, the reader may doubt your ability to do legal analysis. While the rules of citation seem both overwhelming and tedious at first, they can become second nature. Putting a period at the end of a sentence and capitalizing the pronoun "I" are also tedious details of writing in English, but most of us would be suspicious of a legal writer who did not follow those rules.

Despite the many pages of rules in the *Bluebook*, the *ALWD Guide*, Rule 9.800, and the FSM, sometimes you will not be able to find exact instructions or examples for citing your source. When this happens, keep in mind the basic purpose of a citation: to give the reader sufficient information to find the source and verify your analysis as efficiently as possible.

About the Authors

Barbara J. Busharis graduated from NYU School of Law in 1991 and spent three years as an associate with Duane, Morris & Heckscher (now Duane Morris) in Philadelphia. She taught legal writing and research at the Florida State University College of Law from 1994 until 2004. She currently edits the *Trial Advocate Quarterly*, the journal of the Florida Defense Lawyers Association, and is an assistant public defender in Tallahassee, specializing in appeals.

Jennifer Parker LaVia received her JD from the University of Florida in 1987. She began her practice as a full-time trial attorney and later worked for Holland & Knight LLP in Tallahassee, focusing on appellate practice and legal ethics. She has been a member of the faculty at the Florida State University College of Law since 2002. She teaches courses in legal writing and research, professional responsibility, civil rights, and topics in Florida practice.

Suzanne E. Rowe is a 1989 graduate of Columbia University School of Law. After clerking for a federal judge and working with a Wall Street law firm, she taught legal writing and research at the Florida State University College of Law for six years. She is currently the James L. and Ilene R. Hershner Professor at the University of Oregon School of Law, where she directs the legal research and writing program.

Index